SARATOGA
TURNING
POINT

SARATOGA TURNING POINT

The Shot That Gave Birth to a Nation!

ANDREW F. NAZZARO

CITI OF
BOOKS

CITIOFBOOKS, INC.
3736 Eubank NE Suite A1
Albuquerque, NM 87111-3579
www.citiofbooks.com
Hotline: 1 (877) 389-2759
Fax: 1 (505) 930-7244

Ordering Information:
Quantity sales. Special discounts are available on quantity purchases by corporations, associations, and others. For details, contact the publisher at the address above.

Printed in the United States of America.

ISBN-13:   Softcover   979-8-89391-634-8

Library of Congress Control Number: 2025906691

Table of Contents

To my wife, Martha,

to my children,

Maureen Petkiewicz

Andrew G. Nazzaro

and

Philip E. Nazzaro

PREFACE

When I attended grammar school, by sixth or seventh grade we had learned that the Battle of Saratoga was the turning point of the American Revolution, although I wasn't sure what that really meant at the time. That's about all I remembered about it for a long time. I also remembered it occurred sometime around 1776 after the Declaration of Independence was signed but it didn't have much to do with anything in which I was interested at the time. However, a recent trip to the Saratoga Battlefield sparked a renewed interest in the subject and led me to research it further.

The shot that gave birth to a nation, the act on which my story hinges is fact, not fiction. My premise in authoring this novel does not contend that the Battle of Saratoga was turned by a watershed moment as the subtitle might suggest but by a watershed second, or fraction of a second, a single gunshot that turned the tide of the Battle of Saratoga in favor of the Americans, enabling them to defeat the British in this critical battle. Further, it was this single victory that brought France to consider coming to the aid of the Americans as America's first ally which was critical because, without France as an ally, the American patriots would not have won their war for independence.

In my research I discovered a rarely known fact that Timothy Murphy, the person that history contends fired this shot with no primary documentation that can be found even after all these years, may not be the person who fired the shot at all. An article written by noted historian, Hugh T. Harrington addresses this historical twist of fate and was my inspiration for this novel. In it he introduces a different person who contends that he fired the shot of which I speak. He also reveals that it was not until sixty years after the incident that anyone even claimed it was Murphy who fired the shot, and it was the presumed shooter's son who made this claim. The claim that the sharpshooter, Timothy Murphy, was indeed the shooter has been promulgated as fact for more than 175 years simply by it being repeated by historians over and over again.

In my novel, **Saratoga Turning Point**, I have presented my claim as to who fired **the shot that gave birth to a nation,** with as much evidence as historians have given for the person to whom they credit for firing the fateful shot, which is.......**none!**

This novel is a story about this man and what led him to commit this history changing act.

CHAPTER 1

On an early spring day in 1776, Philip Eames drove his wagon down the gentle slope of the road from his small farm and turned north onto the river road. The air was cool, and the sun reflected sharply off the Hudson River which blinked at him like a kaleidoscope through the trees lining its banks. Where he couldn't see the river, the sun flickered between the tree leaves splashing his face alternately with bright light and shade. He wanted to get to Pearson's Mercantile Store five miles up the road in the Saratoga settlement located about 35 miles north of Albany, New York early so he could get back to his farm soon enough to put in a day's work. He needed to pick up the bi-weekly rations and order some cloth for Renee.

Philip, a handsome, well-tanned, well-toned young man with sharp features, just short of six feet tall, pulled up his horse and wagon in front of the store, and he could see he would be the only customer. In fact, he had passed only three people along the way. As he entered the store, the tingling bell above the door broke the stillness and turned the heads of Samuel Pearson behind the counter and his daughter, Martha, at the back stocking shelves.

Martha smiled cheerfully. "Good morning, Philip, so good to see you."

"Heard any of the news from Smythe or Jamieson about what's going on over in Boston, and how some upstarts dumped a shipload of tea in the harbor?" Samuel Pearson, a thin balding man in his sixties with a stern countenance and a slightly hunched posture queried. Smythe and Jamieson traded and carried goods from the region to both Boston and New York City for exportation.

"Can't say that I have, Mr. Pearson. Doesn't matter much to me. My folks were always loyal subjects both here and in England, at least on my father's side, and I have no reason to change that tradition. My father served bravely with the British forces at Ticonderoga, and I will always be proud of his service to the crown."

"You're grown now Philip, how many years have I been asking you to call me Sam?"

"Yes sir, Mr. Pearson....uh...Sam."

"I know your loyalty Philip, but not everyone does. Some folks still don't understand how you could bring back a French girl from up north, and a Catholic at that. So, be careful, you hear?"

"Yes sir, I will. Talk doesn't mean anything to me. You know everyone knows the marriage was arranged, and I have grown to love Renee very much. She is a good wife and mother."

Pearson did not believe for a minute the story about Philip's marriage being arranged. It made no sense at all, an arrangement between an English family and a French Catholic family. He had always hoped that Philip would have taken enough liking to Martha to someday marry her. That would not only have given him a fine son-in-law loyal to the king, but someone to help with the store and a male heir. His wife had died from diphtheria when Martha was a small child, and from that point on Samuel Pearson became bitter and even more humorless than he had always been.

Philip never was very comfortable around Pearson. He seemed such a solemn man who never smiled. Philip tried to imagine how hard it must be to lose a wife at such an early age, but nonetheless, Philip resented that Pearson made him feel obligated to defend his marriage to Renee Merneau, the woman he loved more than life itself. He never felt a need to take such a tact with anyone else, and he would as soon drop a man in his footsteps as look at him if one were to question his choice in a wife or to disparage her in any way. He could not understand this hold Mr. Pearson had over him and resolved to someday somehow rid himself of it. For now, he just did not want to alienate Sam Pearson.

Martha had come over behind the counter and faced Philip with her usual sincere smile. "Philip, how have you been? And how are Renee and young Robert John? Tell Renee she must come into town and bring the children so we can have tea."

"I will, Martha. Good to see you again," replied Philip with a forced smile still thinking about what Sam Pearson had said about his wife.

He was able to stop thinking about it for a minute when he looked at Martha and remembered their youthful relationship. Martha had always been a beautiful girl, but she was a round, soft, chubby child, which perhaps made her easy bait for teasing. But now the roundness and chubbiness had left her, and only the softness and beauty remained. She walked Philip out of the store to his wagon.

"Philip," she implored, "Please do not think ill of my father. He means well. He was much different when my mother was alive. She was the light of his life. She was always so cheerful that she made every day sunny. My father needed her more than any person should need another, and when she died, somehow, I think he felt cheated. I can tell by how he watches other men with their wives. He always stares out the window at them with a soulful look when they leave the store and head home together. I am sure you can understand, especially now that you have Renee. Think of how you would feel, Philip, if someone or something should take her from you."

<hr />

Martha was three years younger than Philip and held a secret admiration, maybe even more than admiration, for Philip in her heart since the time when they attended a small one room schoolhouse together as children. Although she had always liked the quiet and handsome young boy, the feeling grew to its current intensity the time Philip came upon three boys teasing and intimidating her on the way to school one day.

It was a day when she was nine years old, and Philip was eleven. Martha's mother asked Philip's mother if Philip could look after her on the way to and from school. As a result, Philip would ride up to the store each morning on his father's old mare to give Martha a ride to school and return her safely to the store in the afternoon. Philip did not arrive at the usual time on that day, and so, after waiting on the steps in front of the store for about twenty minutes, she feared something may have happened and went into the store to report it to her father. Her father told her to go on by herself on foot, and he would ride out to the Eames place if Philip did not show up soon. As it turned out, the Eames cow had wandered off, and since the early morning milking was Philip's responsibility, he was slowed by the fact that he had to find her first. When he did finally make it to the Pearson's about twenty minutes late, Mr. Pearson told Philip that Martha had gone on ahead. It did not take long for him to catch up to Martha, and when he did, he came upon the scene that had such a lasting impact on Martha. Three boys had engaged hands and encircled Martha. They were shouting insulting phrases, and each time Martha pressured one side of the circle to try to escape, they would push her to the other side. Martha was in tears, being jostled from one side of the circle to the other when Philip arrived. Two of the boys, Philip's friends, were the same age as he. One boy was older, and it was clear that the older boy was the leader and a bully. The older boy was Big Will Stanton who did not attend school with the others but had a reputation for getting his own way through intimidation or by inflicting physical punishment if it came to that. The other boys were Michael Emerson, a boy with a sturdy frame and a big smile about Philip's size, and Peter Framingham, the Anglican minister's son a very bright, quiet, studious boy, tall for his age, but with a slight frame and very much a follower. Peter's father was also the schoolmaster.

"Let her go," Philip shouted. "Peter, this is not like you, and both of you, I'm sure your fathers would not be very proud of you."

"And who put you in charge?" the bully shouted back.

"I did." Philip answered.

"We were just teasing, Philip. Will, can we just forget this? We had our fun," Michael offered.

"Yes, this was wrong," piped in Peter shyly, feeling emboldened by Philip's presence.

"Well, are you prepared to take on the three of us, Will?" asked Philip.

"Yes, and even if I don't fare too well against the three of you, remember there will be a time in the near future when each of you will have to face me alone." With that said, the two younger boys backed up slowly with fear showing on their faces and turned and ran off, leaving Philip to face the older Will.

"Will, we still outnumber you two to one," Philip stated firmly.

"I doubt that little sissy missy will be much help to you."

"You think not? Martha, stop crying and pick up that rock. When I get Will in an advantageous position, hit him in the head with the rock." Philip dismounted and stepped toward Will. Martha stopped crying and picked up the rock. Will turned to watch her pick up the rock, and Philip stepped closer with his fists raised. Will turned back to face Philip.

"Two to one with one with a rock is not a fair fight," Will responded.

"You're right, it's not as fair as one on one while sissy missy watches, but I'm not interested in fairness right now. I'm more interested in teaching you a lesson and putting you in your place. Also, I'm interested in teaching both you and Martha the power of a woman with a weapon."

Once more Will's glance went back and forth between Philip and Martha. Then, after a moment's hesitation, Will leaned forward, and pushing Philip in the chest, turned and sped off in a direction away from the schoolhouse. Philip lifted Martha atop the horse and climbed up behind her. He put his arms around her grasping the reins. Martha relaxed and leaned back against Philip's chest. The feelings she already had for this young man instantly multiplied tenfold. She felt very safe and thought to herself that someday, when she and Philip were grown, he would be the man she would marry.

Philip, Michael, and Peter were about the same age, with birthdays only months apart. They were the only boys in their grade in school and sat in the back row of the room across from each other in the little combination Anglican Church and schoolhouse where all grades were taught in the same room. They had been childhood friends since their first day of school. At morning recess Peter and Michael approached Philip. Michael spoke first.

"Philip, we're terribly sorry. We weren't going to hurt her. We didn't even want to do it but Will....Big Will said he would either beat us or drown us in the river, and he said he wasn't sure which of the two he would do."

"You won't tell my father will you, Philip?" Peter chipped in.

"I won't tell anyone, but you have to make me a promise. If Big Will threatens you again, you must come to me. I'm not sure I can handle him, but for sure together the three of us can."

"We promise...right, Peter?" Michael said with determination in his voice.

"Yes" said Peter shyly, looking down at the ground.

"Give me your hand on it. We have been friends for a long time, and we must stick together," Philip said as he extended his right hand between them face down. Each boy placed his right hand on top of the previous boy's and then did the same with the left. Then they shook the stack of hands up and down and smiled.

"All for one and one for all," Philip said in a firm voice. The boys nodded their heads and looked each other in the eyes with a determined look on their faces.

"All for one, and one for all," they repeated.

"One more thing. You need to apologize to Martha," Philip said. The boys nodded, and Philip summoned Martha to join them from where she was talking with some other girls under a tree. Martha came over to them, and both boys apologized timidly. The bell rang, Martha ran ahead, and the boys walked into the church/schoolhouse, arms across each other's shoulders.

They remained friends from that day on and for the next couple of years Philip rode or walked Martha home from school, leading his horse by his hand, every day until Philip's father left to join the British forces in the French and Indian War. Philip no longer attended school then but worked the farm full time with his mother. Philip continued to see both boys often at the swimming hole in Mill Creek and at Pearson's store and Sunday church services. Michael's father was a farmer and grew wheat and corn. Philip would see Michael often when he and his father brought their harvests to Pearson's to arrange for shipping to Boston or New York with Smythe and Jamieson. Since the Anglican Church was subsidized by the British government, and Peter's father was both the Anglican pastor and teacher, Peter's father only farmed enough for their own personal use.

⸺⁓⸻

The swimming hole at Mill Creek provided the three friends with the only real escape from chores after school and throughout the summer. The boys would plan to meet there at least two to three times a week after school in the late spring and summer. The conversation after school on these days was always pretty much the same.

"Swimming hole today?" Michael would ask.

Peter would nod in agreement.

"Yes" Philip would reply. "You go ahead, and I'll catch up with you in a bit."

Philip would help Martha up behind him on his horse instead of in front of him as she got older and wave to his friends as he rode towards the Pearson's store to return Martha home safely. Michael and Peter would wave back and race for their horses with Michael laughing and shouting about the fun they were about to experience as they went. Philip would lower Martha to the ground and wait for her to safely mount the steps. She would turn and wave, and Philip would wave back and steer his mount in the direction of the swimming hole, advancing the steed in a trot and then a gallop in anticipation of the escape in which he and his friends were about to share.

The swimming hole was approached from a narrow path through the woods that rose over a knoll and then down to the shoreline of the creek. The boys managed to keep the location of their swimming pool private, or so they thought, so that they could engage in skinny dipping without the threat of any unwelcome visitors. They had hung a rope on a branch of an old Oak tree that reached out over the creek at its deepest point. By grabbing hold of the rope from the shore, they could swing out over the creek and let go, dropping into the water feet first. The swing and subsequent drop was always accompanied with a loud scream from Michael and Philip that lasted from the launch until they would hit the water. Of course, Michael's scream was the louder, while Peter's plunge was executed quietly.

Apparently, conversations overheard during school had revealed the existence of their secret rendezvous at the creek. One of the older girls, Sarah Bemis, who preferred to be called Sally, had somehow determined the location of the boys swimming hole. Sally was the freckled, red-headed tomboy daughter of the Bemis Tavern owner, Jotham Bemis. One day in mid-June, the boys were standing waist high in the creek after the last one dropping from the rope had just emerged from the water, pushing his wet hair back from his face. They could hear gentle female laughter coming from over the knoll. Soon, four girls appeared in their view. The boys exchanged looks showing their surprise, dismay, and disapproval as if they had just been invaded by an enemy force.

"What should we do?" asked Michael urgently. Philip and Peter looked at each other quizzically but had no answer.

"Let's show them our arses!" exhorted Michael. Both Philip and Peter nodded approval.

"On three. One...two...three...." shouted Michael. On the count of three with their posteriors facing the girls, all three boys jumped vertically into the air high enough to reveal their buttocks, and then dove headfirst into the water. As the shocked and embarrassed young ladies turned and ran up over the knoll screaming, the boys came out of the water, pushed their hair out of their eyes and smiled victoriously, as they observed the girl's noisy exit. Their leader, Sally Bemis, was unseen as she lagged behind the rest of the girls, hiding behind a tree.

"Come on, Sally," yelled one of the girls.

"Go on, I will be right along," replied Sally, lingering as she watched the boys come out of the water long enough to get the eyeful she had come for.

"One for all and all for one!" shouted Michael as the boys reentered the water and stood waist high in the creek. The boys shook hands, patted each other on their backs, and resumed their private enjoyment of the swimming hole, reassured that such a visit would not be repeated. That was the second time the boys unifying cry had been uttered by them. It would be spoken one last time before they reached adulthood.

About a month after the female invasion of their swimming hole, Peter was swinging on the rope when it broke before reaching the point where one would let go for the drop into the creek. This caused Peter to hit the surface of the water landing on his back. He did not rise above the water in the time it normally would take to do so. Sensing this, both Philip and Michael dove into the water to rescue Peter. Pulling him to the surface, he appeared out of breath, but not much less for wear, neither bruised nor in pain. As he emerged and walked slowly towards the shore with the other boys, he looked side to side speaking to Philip and Michael on his right and left respectively, more embarrassed than hurt and shyly muttered with a smile, "Thanks. All for one. One for all." Philip and Michael nodded agreement and dove into the water. Landing on his back as he struck the surface of the water had simply knocked the wind out of Peter.

"I'm sorry, Martha. I am unjustifiably sensitive. And yes, I do understand now that you put it that way. Thank you for that. Maybe we will all come one day, and while you have tea with Renee, I can fix that shutter your father asked me to tend to."

"I would like that Philip," she said with a look that almost revealed her true feelings. "I really would."

In the back of her mind, she could not help but think that had Philip's parents and her mother lived, a marriage between Philip and her would have been arranged. After all, her father and Philip's father were best friends.

The bell over the door jingled, and Sam Pearson appeared in the doorway.

"Goodbye Martha, Goodbye Mr. Pearson.......uh ... Sam.... uh ...... Sir."

"Goodbye Philip," they both chimed, almost in unison, waving as Philip snapped the reins over his horse's hindquarters.

As he rode back to his farm, Philip's thoughts returned to what Pearson had said about his wife and how he had brought her back from a trapping trip. Although it had happened over two years ago, Pearson could not let go of it, and just the thought of it angered Philip, despite what Martha had said about her father. He thought of his beloved Renee and how he came to meet her. From the day he saw her for the first time, under what most would agree were most unusual circumstances, he felt somehow that he was meant to share his life with her.

CHAPTER 2

It was a clear crisp fall morning in October of 1775, when Philip Eames rode into a clearing at a mountain top to the east of Lake George. You could see for over a hundred miles with Lake George glistening below as the sun broke through the trees. The view was panoramic and the colors magnificent. Philip sat astride his horse as he scanned the landscape from left to right, and back again. He breathed deeply. The air was cold and crisp, and through his breath which trailed off in a wisp as he exhaled, he admired the beauty and color of the fall leaves. The reds, yellows, oranges, burgundies, and golds reflected the sun's light and overcame one's sense of sight. Aligning the lake, groves of silver fir, white pine, aspen, and paper birch trees reached down to the water's edge with precipices of rock checkering the scene. He thought of his mother who always reflected on the brilliance of the New York fall compared to the drab yellow color of the leaves during the fall in England. At the southern end of Lake George stood the site of Fort William Henry. Just beyond the charred remains of the fort which was burned by the French during the French and Indian War, on the southeastern side of the lake, a trail of smoke rose into the sky, interrupting the stillness of nature's landscape picture below. The volume of smoke indicated the source was bigger than a chimney or campfire, and Philip decided he would take a detour on his way home to Saratoga to investigate.

Philip began his descent from the high plateau, working his way toward the source of the smoke. He rode through woods on trails he had followed many times before, but had to walk, leading his horse as he cut his way through the underbrush where trails did not exist. At times the brush was so thick that he lost sight of the smoke, but he would work his way to a clearing to search for it so he could confirm that he was taking the most direct route possible. After about six hours, late in the afternoon, he emerged from the woods at the source of the smoke into a clearing where he witnessed a grizzly scene.

Charred remains smoldered where a cabin once stood. Now, only the fireplace and chimney remained. At first, he saw no signs of life. Then he thought he heard a voice. His eyes scanned the clearing. Within fifty feet of the cabin, a young woman of about nineteen or twenty years of age was leaning over the form of another woman lying next to a large fallen tree trunk. Philip's boot stepped on a small branch on the ground, snapping and revealing his presence to the young woman. Quickly, instinctively, she reached for the rifle at her side, directing it toward Philip. Her face was filled with fear, and she was breathing in short breaths as if gasping for air. Philip approached slowly, raising his hand as if to shield himself from a shot from the rifle.

"Please," he said, "I won't hurt you. I saw the smoke and I came to help."

For a reason she could not explain, she believed him. It was something in the kindness that showed through his eyes perhaps, or something about his quiet, deliberate approach.

"What happened?"

"Indians," she replied, as she rose and let the rifle fall. Anguish showed on her face. As she looked down at the woman on the ground beneath her, she raised her hand to push back her long black wavy tresses from her face with tears streaming down her cheeks. Even through the tears and ashes streaked her face, Philip could tell she was unbelievably beautiful. Her forehead was high, her dark eyes large and round. Her cheek bones were high, and her nose and chin small, all well-proportioned, framing her full lips. She was about five feet four inches tall, about six inches shorter than him. She had a small slender frame and wore a long full dress that gathered at the waist hugging her tiny waist tightly. "They killed my father and perhaps my mother." Her voice revealed a French accent.

Philip, intuitively concluding the woman on the ground, barely breathing, was the mother of the young woman, he asked, "Where is your father?"

"Over there," she said, pointing to a spot some fifty yards away where a mix of fresh earth and stones rose about twelve inches above the ground, identifying a recently covered makeshift grave. A big red and black mixed breed short haired dog was lying beside the grave.

"I am sure the grave is not adequate but that was the best I could do. His dog will not leave his grave. He was always by his side, both day and night."

"What did he call his dog?"

"Soldat, French for Soldier. He certainly has been a good soldier to my father."

Philip tried to attract the dog away from the grave by calling his name. Soldat turned toward Philip. His ears perked up at the sound of his name, but he would not budge so much as an inch.

"Your father died in the fire?"

"No, the Indians killed him. Yesterday he was chopping wood, and they shot him with an arrow from the woods over there. I watched from the cabin. And then...then they scalped him," she said sobbing."

She described a scene all too familiar to Philip. There were three Indians at the edge of the woods. One had let out a war cry, and launching an arrow from his bow, had shot the young woman's father in the chest. As he fell landing face up, another Indian rushed him, striking him on the head with his tomahawk. After two or three blows, he quickly drew his knife, and while hunched over him, made an incision around the hair from the upper part of the forehead to the back of the neck. Then he turned his victim over face down, arose to his feet, put his foot on his shoulders, and pulled the hair off with both hands, from front to back.

When she had finished her story, she buried her head in Philip's chest as she sobbed. He put his arms around her, and Philip had the feeling that he had known this woman forever. He thought to himself, I don't even know her name.

"My name is Philip.......Philip Eames. I am a trapper from Saratoga."

"I am Renee Merneau. My father was Robert." She took his hand, leading him. "Come....my mother. She is awfully bad. She breathed much smoke during the fire."

She bent over her mother, whose eyes were closed. She was in and out of consciousness, and her breathing was very shallow. She tried to comfort her, adjusting a blanket around her, speaking to her softly in French, and attempting to give her a sip of water from a cup.

"How did the fire start?" Philip asked.

"I believe the Indians started it also," she replied.

Philip was somewhat perplexed. Indian raids had diminished measurably over the past twenty years. In addition, anyone living here in the wilderness for any period survived by making peace with local tribes and developed and nurtured an ongoing relationship.

"Did your father have a problem with the Indians in the area," he asked.

"No, not for many years, but lately there was a dispute over traps, I believe. A few weeks ago, three Indians approached my father here outside the cabin, and voices were raised. He said the Indians claimed he was encroaching on their trapping area, but my father said he had been trapping in the same area for twenty years. They left, but I could tell my father was upset. He said he was not about to change what he had been doing for twenty years. He was a proud and stubborn man.... and very independent. That night, after I buried my father, the cabin was set on fire. When I awoke, flames were all about me. I quickly took as many things as possible...blankets and clothes...that I could carry and I rushed outside to breathe some fresh air and to see who had started the fire, but they were gone. By then, the cabin was completely on fire, and I did not see my mother anywhere. I called her name and then realized she must still be in the cabin. I rushed inside to find her. I had to come out again...I could not breathe. I covered my mouth and crawled back inside to my mother's bedside. She was still in the bed, gasping. She lost consciousness, but I was able to drag her out of the cabin. It seemed to take forever. I was able to start a small fire with wood from the shed."

She pointed to a small woodshed some twenty yards off. "We fell asleep here next to this fallen tree."

Her eyes directed Philip's view to the large fallen oak tree trunk just beside her mother's form near the edge of the clearing.

"We have been here the entire day with nothing to eat. My mind told me to go down to the settlement by the lake and ask someone for help, but I could not leave my mother. I thought that we would surely starve."

"I have food," Philip replied. "Here, take my pack," he said as he lifted his supplies from the back of his horse. "There are blankets and a bear fur also. It will be dark soon. I will gather some pine needles to prepare a more comfortable bed for you and your mother. Then we must start a new fire. It will be dark soon, and cold. Is there somewhere we can get water?"

"Yes. There is a stream over there," she said, pointing.

Philip retrieved some blackened pots and utensils from the ashes, and then disappeared into the woods in the direction that Renee had pointed. In about twenty minutes he returned with the pots and utensils that he had cleaned in the stream. He disappeared once more and returned with a kettle of water. A third time he entered the woods with a blanket and returned with it bursting with pine needles. When he returned, Renee had a fire going with wood from the shed and had a kettle beginning to boil. They prepared tea and dined on jerky. Renee made a broth from the jerky and boiling water which she fed to her mother as she slipped into and out of consciousness, coughing and wheezing. They prepared the beds of pine needles and lifted Renee's mother onto one as gently as possible.

"Tomorrow, I will get some fresh meat for us," Philip said apologetically.

"This is fine, you have been very kind."

As darkness settled in, Philip and Renee leaned against the tree trunk gazing thoughtfully at the fire.

"Who are you, Philip? I know you are Philip Eames, but you know what I mean. Tell me about this Philip Eames. Where is he from? What does he do? Does he have a family, a mother, a father?"

With Renee having known him for only a few hours, Philip was somewhat surprised that she was so interested in him and his family. He had never known anyone like this young woman before, and he had never shared his story with anyone. This is a very unusual young woman, he thought, as he told Renee about how his parents had come to this country from England and about his own life up to the present.

CHAPTER 3

Philip's father, John, came to America to start a new life in 1749, but not because of any religious oppression in England like so many others. His father's family were Anglicans and always fiercely loyal subjects to the king. His father was a blacksmith just outside of London, and in fact did a good business tending to the horses of the royal cavalry. Late in the 1740's, the soldiers began telling John that there were increasing problems with the French in the colonies, and increased military activity there might see some of them being sent to the New York colony on assignment. When some of the men whose horses he smithed no longer came to him, upon inquiring, he learned that they indeed had been sent to the colonies. John, on his own for several years after the death of his parents, decided to enlist in the British Army if he could be allowed to serve in the British colonial army in New York. His request was granted, and within a week he boarded a ship to seek his fortune and adventure in the new world.

Philip's mother's background was quite different from his fathers, and it is quite unusual that she ended up married to his father considering it. His mother, Helen Caldwell, was a Quaker and a member of a large family contingent taking the bold step of moving to the colonies to escape the oppression under which they lived in England. She was a young girl of sixteen, and her parents were not part of the family group she was with on the ship, having died a few years ago of a mysterious illness that swept her village and many neighboring villages. She was traveling with her aunt, her mother's sister, who had taken her in when her mother and father died.

She met Philip's father on the ship on the journey across the ocean, and Helen and John, both very young and on their own, and perhaps lonely as well, became acquainted very quickly in the close quarters of the ship and fell in love. When they had almost reached the colonies, and her family was readying themselves to embark on the journey to their destination in Pennsylvania to join other Quakers, Helen announced to them that she would marry John Eames, not only not a Quaker, but an Anglican at that. They were shocked because John and Helen had been able to keep their ship romance a secret so well. Helen's family initially did not take the news well and warned her of the dire consequences she was about to face at the hands of an Anglican husband, but Helen remained steadfast in her decision to marry John.

Philip's mother had often talked to him as a child about a side of her family who long ago had been pirates on the high seas, and Philip, after hearing about his parents' love story from his mother, always surmised that it must been that side of the family that she favored since she was bold enough to go against her family and marry his father. The marriage of an Anglican to a Quaker was especially bold considering the time in history when this occurred, when arranged marriages were the most widely accepted method of taking on a spouse. The lack of well-established social customs in the colonies, unless you were a member of the old English aristocracy, would make such a move somewhat easier than had it occurred in the mother country.

Along with her initial disapproval, her aunt was reluctant to let her only sister's daughter fare for herself in a strange new land. Thus, Helen was able to convince her aunt to support her decision and to allow her to stay with her in Pennsylvania as originally planned for the duration of her husband-to-be's enlistment. So, with her extended family as reluctant witnesses, the ship's captain married the young couple.

For most of John's enlistment, his primary duty assignment was to serve the British army as a blacksmith, visiting his wife whenever the opportunity presented itself. Philip Eames was born in 1750 and stayed with his mother and her aunt until his father was released from the army in 1761. Only once was he called upon to serve in combat where he did so with valor while reporting to a Captain Philip Schuyler. Philip Schuyler was born in Albany to a wealthy colonial family. The Schuylers had gradually expanded their holdings and influence in the New World. Schuyler joined the British forces in 1755 during the French and Indian War, raised a company, and was commissioned as a captain. In July of 1758, a devastating defeat occurred for Schuyler's forces where nearly two thousand men lost their lives during a frontal attack from Lake George, against well entrenched French forces at Fort Ticonderoga. Philip's father performed heroically, and returned home a second lieutenant, having received a battlefield commission on the recommendation of Captain Schuyler.

When his enlistment was up, John joined his wife in Pennsylvania where he was able to secure a small piece of land with the money he had saved while in the army where he built a cabin and served the Quaker community as a blacksmith. Although he never became a member of the Society of Friends himself, he followed their customs and traditions in support of his wife.

Then, one day in 1761, John received a letter from his longtime friend, Samuel Pearson, who reported to John that a few years ago he and his wife had taken positions in Albany, New York with a Mr. Philip Schuyler where they were to work on his estate for seven years in exchange for transportation from England to Albany, food, clothing, and shelter. Further he announced to John in his letter that Mr. Schuyler had purchased several thousand acres of land about 35 miles north of the city where he was investing a great deal of money to develop the area and that he had offered him the position of running a general store there. Sam said in the letter that he had accepted the offer and implored John to follow him and his wife, certain that this new settlement called Saratoga would need a good blacksmith. If they would join him and his wife, also a childhood friend of John's, John and his wife could stay with them temporarily until they could find a place of their own. Remembering Captain Schuyler as the man under whom he had served valiantly and acknowledging the opportunity seemingly available in this new settlement, John convinced Helen that they should join his close friend, Sam Pearson, and his wife in Saratoga.

In the early part of the eighteenth century, the northeast region of North America remained much as it had been for centuries. French trappers and backwoodsmen from Canada and their English counterparts from the British colonies traveled through its woods and rivers, but the principal occupants of the region were Native Americans and a greatly diverse wildlife. As the British colonies became more populated and prosperous, life became more agrarian in the countryside and more stable and commercial in the cities. Colonial governments became more formalized, and northeastern cities became more populated.

The settlement known as Saratoga, located about 35 miles north of Albany, was approximately150 miles north of New York City. It was bounded on the east by the river road running along the western bank of the Hudson River which flowed in a north-south direction for the full 13 miles of the settlement and beyond to where it originated at Tear Lake of the Clouds some 72 miles north in the Appalachian Mountains.

To the west, the settlement stretched about five and a half miles at its widest point. The river road connected the properties of the settlers from the Bemis Tavern at the southernmost point to the Marshall farm at the northern most point. The tavern sat below a hill on the Bemis property just to the north of it known as Bemis Heights. At the highest point on "The Heights," as it was called, sat a plateau which commanded a view of a good portion of the farming area occupying the lower third of the settlement. Facing north from its summit, The Heights overlooked the Neilson farm, the Freeman farm, the Barber farm, the Chatfield farm, and almost to the Sword farm. The Marshall farm was well out of sight at the far end of the settlement a little over ten miles north of the Sword farm.

Just a little over two miles south of the Marshall farm and about eight miles north of the Sword farm was the Schuyler property, the summer home of Philip Schuyler. The Schuylers, descendants of wealthy Dutch immigrants owned 24,000 acres in the Saratoga area through inheritance from Philip's grandfather to Philip's father, and ultimately to Philip Schuyler, as well as a mansion in Albany which sat on 80 acres overlooking the Hudson River. Built in the 1760's, Philip Schuyler turned the Saratoga property into a busy farming, milling, and merchandising center, worked by tenants, enslaved people, and artisans who also lived, for the most part, between the Schuyler property and the Sword farm. The Schuyler farm grew wheat, flax, and hemp crops and included a linen mill, sawmills, a herring fishery, and a general store run by Samuel Pearson, selling goods and services.

The general store was located about halfway between the Schuyler property and the Sword farm on the west side of the river road. Although owned by Schuyler, the store carried the Pearson name. In addition to serving the material needs of its customers, it also served their commercial needs and as a hub for the exporting of the local trappers' pelts and the settlers' farm products and the importing of goods from England and the rest of Europe through New York City and Boston. As one might expect, with no newspaper in the immediate area, it came to serve also as a social gathering place for the locals to keep abreast of news from the colonies, the mother country, and the rest of Europe.

⸺◦⸺

Once arriving in Saratoga, John Eames and his wife stayed with the Pearson's until John was able to secure a small tenant farm just a mile or so south of the general store and about three miles north of the Sword farm. The barn at the rear of the Eames house also served as home to John Eames' blacksmith shop. Nearby merchants often told John that he should move his shop to a more populated area of the colony, but he would not hear of it. He preferred the closeness of his friend, Sam Pearson, the freedom of the country and his little farm where he could grow food for his family and have a couple of farm animals, which helped him become more self-sufficient.

John and Helen were happy on their small tenant farm raising vegetables and wheat. Aside from the family horse and a work horse, they had a cow for milk, a sheep for wool, and a dog that kept watch over Philip as a baby and slept on the fireplace hearth where he could keep watch on the door. The barn, which housed stables for the horses, the cow, and the sheep had space for food, both for the family and the animals, and also housed the blacksmith shop. The land, of course, was owned by their landlord, Philip Schuyler. They were able to supply much of their vegetable needs from the farm, trading their surplus crops for those things they could not produce to his friend Sam Pearson who used them to feed his family and to stock his store. In addition, proceeds from the blacksmith shop supplied the family with additional income and was a stabilizing factor during those years when poor weather limited the output of the farm. Helen worked alongside of her husband on the farm until Philip was born, and, after a brief period of maternity recovery, joined him again, bringing infant Philip to the farm fields with her. As a baby, Philip would lie in a basket under a tree between feedings, and then amuse himself on a blanket as he got older.

When Philip was old enough to attend school but was not yet old enough to help with the smithing, his father John had taken on an apprentice, Drew Gerard, a young man a few years older than Philip, who no longer attended school, but read everything he could get his hands on whenever Philip's father gave him a break from the grueling work in the shop.

Philip's father also worked from time to time on Mr. Schuyler's country estate. At about the same time, when Philip was a boy of eleven, his father would take him on hunting trips occasionally. It was on these trips that Philip discovered his love of the wild. John Eames taught his young son how to make snares and set a trap line and how to stalk and hunt deer. He learned how to survive in the wild through all seasons. His father taught Philip how to tan the hide of a deer by soaking Hemlock bark chips in water and then soaking the hides in the brown soupy liquid. He learned which berries, roots, seeds, nuts, and tree barks could be harvested to eat and which plants made a stomach-warming tea. Philip could not help but think of how the forest seemed to be a world of its own. There were times while walking quietly by his father's side that he felt he could hear the forest breathe.

Philip would attend church services often with his father on Sunday and tried awfully hard to listen to Pastor Framingham's sermons, not always with success. Additionally, however, he was tutored in the beliefs and customs of the Quakers by his mother at home. He tried hard to remain faithful to both religious influences. But always feeling called by the forest while working on the farm, he would longingly look forward to hunting trips with his father.

He always felt closer to God at the crest of a hill, or surrounded by a forest deep in the wilderness, or along a rushing brook, all untouched by human hands.

Suddenly, one day in 1763, the same year the Treaty of Paris officially ending the French and Indian War was signed, Philip's father did not return from a hunting trip on which Philip had not accompanied him. He was found lying dead in the woods by some trappers. Philip could not help but wonder if he could had saved his father somehow if he had only been with him. After some thought, he came to realize that it probably would not have made a difference because his father had not been wounded. There was not a mark found on his body. It seemed that his heart had simply stopped beating.

Philip had never really taken to smithing, so when John Eames died, Drew took over the business. Drew took Philip under his wing and passed on to him much wisdom. Now, Philip's role in the farm work became more important. The farm, along with his mother's sewing were the only means of support for a while. Eventually, she would also work in the kitchen of Mr. Schuyler's country home. Each evening, Philip and his mother would load up the wagon with vegetables from the previous day's harvest and bring them, along with any sewing his mother had done, to the Pearson's home behind the store the following morning. Philip and the Pearson's daughter, Martha, would walk from there to school and back. In the afternoon, Sam Pearson would bring Philip home in his wagon and deliver any goods that his mother may have ordered that morning. By the time Philip was eleven years old, he would drive the family wagon himself to the Pearson's and take Martha back and forth to school with him. Eventually, these trips back and forth to school would be made on horseback. It also became his job to take his father's place by meeting with Mr. Schuyler to reconcile the entries in the books which recorded the deliveries he made to him and accounted for the fifteen percent owed him for the privilege of working the little tenant farm.

On his first such visit, as was so in every visit that followed, as Philip was tethering his horse to the hitching post, he saw Caleb, one of General Schuyler's slaves kneeling at a flower garden at the side of the house cultivating a flower bed. Caleb was the name given to him by the general when he arrived from Africa. His given name was Mutombo, which meant faithful. He had been appointed to this envious position because of his connection to Anna, his wife, also a slave and a member of the household staff. As Philip was walking up the path to the house, Caleb rose to his feet and approached him.

"Master Philip?"

"Yes."

"I am Caleb. General Schuyler asked me to be a look out for you. He must like you, Master Philip. He sure was happy and smiling really big when he was a telling me about you coming. Come this way," Caleb replied in his stilted English.

"Caleb, I am pleased to meet you." Caleb led Philip to the door, knocked to announce his arrival and opened the door.

Philip was met at the door by Miss Dorothy, as she was called, a large framed white haired matronly woman with rosy cheeks and a broad smile, who oversaw the female staff of the Schuyler's family home. She had such a love for flowers that there always was a vase of fresh flowers from her garden in every room. Miss Dorothy led him to a small office in the rear of the house.

"Make yourself comfortable. Mr. Schuyler will be with you momentarily," she said as she exited, closing the door behind her.

Philip sat quietly for a few moments, and then, becoming restless, he started to peruse the books from a bookcase which occupied the top half of one wall of the room. As he found a book of interest, he placed it on a small circular table below the bookcase. Then he sat in the chair by the table and began to read. After the better part of thirty minutes had passed, the door opened, and Schuyler entered. Philip closed the book he had been reading, placed it next to a second book on the table, and rose to his feet in respect. General Schuyler was tall, slender, and stood very erect. His piercing eyes resembled that of a hawk and matched his dark hair, while his nose resembled a hawk's beak. His complexion was ruddy, and his countenance reflected his feeling of confidence and superiority. One might say his appearance even seemed haughty and arrogant.

"Sit down, sit down, young Eames," Schuyler said as he walked around his desk and sat down. "So, young man, I understand from your mother that you are my namesake."

"Yes, sir, my father had much admiration for you."

"As I did for him. He served in the Northern Campaign with valor and bravery. It is something a commanding officer never forgets. I was saddened to hear about his death. And how is your mother holding up?"

"Thank you, sir. She is taking it hard, but I believe she will be able to bear up."

Opening the top drawer of the desk and withdrawing a piece of parchment, he handed it to young Philip.

"I believe this may well make things easier for the both of you."

Looking down and reading the parchment, Philips eyes widened. Looking up, with his mouth open, searching for words, this young quiet natured boy could say nothing.

"It is a deed to the land your family works," Schuyler said with a rare smile. "It is your mothers until you come of age, and then it is yours with the provision that your mother shall live there until she joins your father."

"Thank you, sir, but I have no way to........."

"Do not thank me, Schuyler interrupted, turn your eyes to the heavens and thank your father. He more than earned it."

Before Philip could say anything, Schuyler's eyes turned to the books on the table as he rose from behind the desk, and young Philip rose as well.

"I see you have met my friends, Plato, Mr. Locke and Monsieur Descartes. Take them along with you. They will be your mentors, teach you how to think, and you will take comfort in their words forever."

Then he went to the bookshelf and took down works by Socrates and Aristotle and a copy of *King Arthur and the Knights of the Round Table.*

"And take these along as well. Socrates and Aristotle influenced both Locke and Descartes, and King Arthur is for entertainment and to build your character as well."

Then, putting his hand on young Philip's shoulder, Schuyler opened the door and ushered his young visitor out.

―――

On his return home, Philip stopped in the barn that still served as Drew's black smithing shop as he often did, just for a short visit. Although he did not initially say anything, Drew noticed the books Mr. Schuyler had given Philip under his arm. Philip was always welcome, and as they talked, Drew usually passed on some local hearsay or rumor just to make idol conversation. As Philip grew older, in such a situation he would not only listen to Drew but take a position in discussions with him.

On this occasion, in response to a local rumor passed on by Drew, Philip stated, Descartes would tell you to never take as true anything you did not know to be true by evidence of which you are personally aware and to not pass judgment based on the words of others.

Drew smiled, considering such a comment from young Philip as somewhat precocious.

"So, who is this Descartes, and how do you know of him?"

"He was a French philosopher. Mr. Schuyler just gave me an English translation of one of his books that I read while I was waiting for him in his library."

Philip brought forth the philosophy books given to him by Philip Schuyler and he and Drew browsed them together, reading and commenting on brief passages as they did so. From that point on, Drew borrowed Philip's books often until he could get copies of his own. Drew's knowledge of what these philosophers professed soon paralleled Philips, and they would pass many hours discussing the exciting ideas they discovered between the pages of Plato, Aristotle, Socrates, Descartes, and Locke.

―――

Despite his father's death, Philip was rather happy during this period, but when he was fifteen years old, his life suddenly changed again. Philip's mother contracted smallpox and died after only a few weeks, almost exactly two years after his father had passed. The Pearsons took Philip in for awhile, and he helped around the store, but the life of a storekeeper was not for him. He became bored with such an existence. The news from Boston and New York brought back by Smythe and Jamieson, however, broke the monotony and engendered lively discussions when the men would gather around to hear the news or read the month-old newspapers the traders had brought with them.

Philip's school friend, Peter Framingham, would accompany his father to the Pearson's store, and on the occasions when such news generated lively discussions with strong views on both sides, Philip could see that Peter was truly in his element. Not inclined to say much, but also not allowed by the men to speak because of his youthful age, Peter could only listen attentively, but Philip could see the excitement in his eyes. Philip looked forward to these occasional visits from his old school friend. He remembered Peter as the brightest student in school and often shared his philosophy books with him, as he had done with Drew.

Peter did not express his opinion very often because he was not inclined to argue, but he felt very comfortable around Philip. Feeling that Philip was more open minded than Michael, he was more open with Philip when Michael was not around. Peter especially liked Locke, and using much of Locke's logic, he would press Philip to agree with the colonists view regarding no taxation without representation. Philip was not as moved as Peter, not being as interested as he of things of a political nature and remembering his father's loyalty to the crown. He did not express a contrary view with his friend, but neither did he necessarily agree. He was more concerned that Peter had borrowed his book by Locke for such a long time that he feared he would never see it again. Then one day Peter returned it very apologetically and arranged for Mr. Pearson to get him his own copy from England.

After situations such as this, Philip would seek out his friend and surrogate big brother, Drew Gerard, to find someone to lend a sympathetic ear. Drew had no reason to feel empathy toward the British and was simply as apolitical, if not more so, as he. They both agreed that much was owed to Britain for what they had done for the colonies, and so, after a few brief moments reinforcing each other's conservative views, they spent the rest of the time discussing philosophy, something they both enjoyed much more than politics.

Philip began helping the other settlers in the area with carpentry work. He found this more interesting than store keeping and eventually became quite accomplished. But most of all, Philip still preferred the solitude of the woods, escaping to the solace they provided as often as possible. By the time he was sixteen, he returned to the farm to live, but began trapping more and more, venturing farther and farther into the woods. Soon he would be gone on trapping trips for weeks or even months at a time, returning home only to sell his furs. Then after resting for a few weeks, he would pack up his horse with supplies along with his philosophy books and return to the forest. By the time he was eighteen years old he had become what was known as a true long-hunter.

He could travel hundreds of miles through the woods using natural features such as streams and trees as guideposts. Philip developed a keen sense of smell and a heightened sense of hearing and sight. He could identify different animals by their hoof or footprints and droppings and then follow their trail through the dense undergrowth of the forest and along stream banks using such evidence, as well as that provided by damaged tree branches and undergrowth, to reveal their path. He had learned from his father how to quickly build a shelter from the natural materials the woods had to offer. He could build a lean-to from tree branches with a roof of pine boughs and a bed of pine needles. He often sought the protection of a cave or earthen bank facing south in order to break the cold north winds at night and draw heat from the sun during the day. He could kill and skin a bear and tan its hide to make a thick warm winter blanket or coat or kill and tan a deer's hide into a fringed leather shirt, pants, and moccasins. Often, he salted and smoked deer meat strips over the fire to sustain himself on those days when the kill was sparse or secondary to his trapping efforts. He learned an important rule of survival was to build a relationship with the Indians, which was not always an easy thing to do. Philip attempted to accomplish this by sharing his venison, and even sometimes the hides of the animals he trapped. In turn the Indians taught him how to handle and throw a tomahawk and a knife with skill and precision. Despite this, Philip was never completely sure that his trust was fully returned, and therefore he was always wary of his Indian neighbors. Finally, however, there was a single event which cemented a relationship of mutual trust with them more than any of the things he had done in the past.

On an autumn trapping excursion, while riding his horse deep into the woods, at the foot of a cliff no less than forty feet in height, he came upon a young unconscious Iroquois native lying face down. Apparently, he had fallen from the cliff and sustained some degree of injury that Philip could not immediately determine. He dismounted, cautiously turned the Indian on his back, and placed his ear near his mouth to ascertain if he was breathing. Discovering that he was, Philip wrapped him in a blanket and built a fire. After a vigil of several hours, the Indian gained consciousness and Philip fed him some warm rabbit broth. Philip's patient soon was able to communicate to Philip that his leg was in pain. Upon examination, Philip determined that the leg was fractured, and he prepared a splint. For several days, Philip would leave his patient by the fire and go off into the woods to set new traps and check others previously set. After several days, Philip was able to lift the young Indian up on his horse and lead him to his tribal camp under the young native's direction. Philip was welcomed with appreciation and was treated as a guest with food, drink, and the sharing of a peace pipe before he went on his way.

For almost ten years, from 1766 to1775, Philip's life was that of the long-hunter. During this period, Philip remained almost oblivious to what was going on in the more civilized part of the colonial world about him. It was only on his occasional trips to the Pearson's to deliver his pelts for shipping abroad and to pay his respect to Martha and her father, or to have a brief visit with Drew and his old school friends, Michael, and Peter, that he learned what was going on in the colonies during this period of growing volatility. Each time he concluded that this was not his world, and he was always happy to escape to the world of the wilderness that he knew and loved.

CHAPTER 4

The Seven Years War was a global war that included several European powers and could probably be called the First World War. It was principally a struggle for global primacy between Britain and France. The war in Europe aligned Britain and Prussia against France and Austria. The Treaty of Hubertusburg of 1763 ended the war between Austria and Prussia, but the greatest impact of the treaty was that it signified the rise of Britain as a world power. The Anglo Prussian victory resulted in many territorial changes beyond the European continent but had no effect on territorial changes on the continent itself, returning all territorial control there to the "status quo ante bellum," the situation that existed before the war.

The Seven Years War on the North American continent was known as the French and Indian War. The war in America was basically a dispute over the control of the upper Ohio River valley between England and France. Settlers on the American continent began to look towards the lands across the Appalachian Mountains as providing new opportunities for settlement and economic growth. The French claimed the entire watersheds of the Mississippi and St. Lawrence Rivers, including the Great Lakes and the Ohio River Valley. They became worried about British encroachments into this region and so set up a series of forts at Crown Point on Lake Champlain, and on the Wabash, Ohio, Mississippi, and Missouri Rivers, as well as others. The British built forts at Oswego and Halifax. To encourage growth in the area, the government granted lands in the Ohio Valley to the Ohio Company and traders set up bases in the region. The territory involved was claimed by the French. Britain, on the contrary, claimed the territory as part of the British Empire, open to settlement by the colonies of Virginia and Pennsylvania. At the heart of the dispute was the control of territory, waterways, beaver trade, and Indian fur trade.

In addition, many of the British settlers objected to France's presence on the continent on religious grounds. The protestant British settlers saw the control of France's land on the continent as controlled by France and the Roman Catholic Church and thus a threat to their religious freedom and customs under English law. The protestant British clergy considered it a religious war, claiming the Catholic French to be the "Mother of Harlots" in reference to the Papacy.

The Treaty of Paris of 1763 ended the French and Indian War between France, Britain, and Spain with the drawing of territorial lines largely in favor of Britain. In signing the treaty, France relinquished all its territories in mainland North America. Britain recovered Florida and Canada and ceded Louisiana to Spain.

The Seven Years War in Europe and the French and Indian War in the colonies' exhausted England's treasury. In seeking relief from its huge national debt, England felt expecting the colonists to help with taxes was justified since tax rates in the mother country were higher than tax rates in the colonies.

In 1764, the English Parliament passed the Sugar Act increasing duties on imported sugar and other items, doubled the duties on foreign goods re-shipped from England to the colonies and forbade the importing of foreign rum and French wines. In May, at a town meeting in Boston, distinguished attorney, James Otis, one of the most influential men in the colonies, raised the issue of taxation without representation in the Massachusetts Assembly, a phrase which would be repeated hundreds of times as the feelings of opposition to British rule in the colonies continued to grow. John Adams, a political activist from Massachusetts, later declared that on that day "the child Independence was born." In July, Otis published *The Rights of the British Colonies Asserted and Proved*. Boston merchants boycotted many British goods the following month.

Later that same year, Britain passed the Currency Act invalidating any legal tender paper money issued by the colonies. Feeling that such a move further threatened the colonial economy, the colonists became further united in their opposition to the British government.

In March of the following year, the Stamp Act passed by the English Parliament imposed the first direct tax ever on the American colonies. This would be the first time Americans would pay tax directly to England. In order to offset the high costs of the British military organization in America, this act taxed all printed materials. Those most affected by the Act, lawyers, publishers, landowners, ship builders and merchants, led the opposition. Opposition to the Stamp Act went very quickly from a vocal stage to an active one. In May of 1764 Patrick Henry as a member of the Virginia House of Burgesses presented seven resolutions to that body. Formalizing Otis' position of no taxation without representation, among the resolutions was the declaration that only the Virginia assembly could legally tax Virginia residents. He vowed, "If this be treason, make the most of it." As a result, the Sons of Liberty was formed in several colonial towns in opposition to the Stamp Act. All the British stamp agents were forced to resign, and many American merchants stopped ordering British goods.

The Sons of Liberty was founded by Samuel Adams, second cousin to John Adams and a member of the Massachusetts House of Representatives, to advance the rights of the colonists and to fight taxation and other intrusive and unfair laws imposed on the thirteen colonies. Their initial activities included public demonstrations and publication of pamphlets against British rule. As time went on, they became increasingly impatient and concluded, as most, that actions would speak louder than words. Their actions expanded to include the destruction of Crown goods and property, and even at times, the tar and feathering of outspoken Loyalists.

In October, nine of the colonies sent representatives to the Stamp Act Congress in New York City as a committee to prepare a resolution petitioning King George and the English Parliament to repeal the Stamp Act and the Sugar Act. The petition repeated the assertion by Patrick Henry that only colonial legislatures can tax the colonies and that taxation without representation violated the colonists' civil rights. On the day when the Stamp Act was to go into effect, most daily business and legal transactions in the colonies came to a halt. Mobs harassed British troops and looted houses. Many of the more prosperous citizens opposed the strong-armed taxes of the Sons of Liberty, preferring instead to simply pay the taxes imposed by Britain.

———

This was the view shared by Philip's friend, Michael Emerson, whom he met, along with Peter Framingham, at a quite improbable meeting at the Bemis Tavern. It was quite uneventful for Philip, but somewhat of a rite of passage for his childhood friends as it was their first such trip. At sixteen years of age, with no drinking age laws or restrictions at the time, and no parents to whom he was accountable, Philip was quite free to make all decisions relative to social behavior and such in the manner of an adult. That, however, was not the case for Michael and Peter. On a day after returning from a hunting and trapping trip, Philip decided that he deserved a refreshing pint of ale. Philip was surprised however to see Michael and Peter at the tavern. They had just finished helping Peter's father make some modest repairs to the church/schoolhouse and came to the same conclusion as did Philip. It was Michael's idea, as one might expect, to take this risky step, fully aware that word might get back to his father should he be seen by one of his father's friends or acquaintances. Being the more adventurous of the two, he was more ready to take such a chance than Peter, feeling that it would be easier to beg for forgiveness than to ask for permission from his father. Through much convincing and cajoling, Peter reluctantly agreed to go along.

As they sat at a table in the tavern early in November, the talk was of the Sons of Liberty and their rioting and constant physical harassment of the British over the British laws placed on the colonies. Their conversation was interrupted by Jotham Bemis' daughter, Sally, approaching the young men. Philip remembered Sally from his schooldays as one of the older girls, but never knew that she was the one who had led the raid on him and his friends at their swimming hole on Mill Creek. He also knew that there was a personal relationship between her and Drew Gerard because, on his first trip to the tavern in which he was accompanied by Drew, Drew had gone behind the bar to engage in a private conversation with her. Sally had now lost her freckles and had become a stunning, shapely, red-haired, green-eyed woman with a well-toned athletic frame.

"Hello, gentlemen. Philip, good to see you again. I remember you came in with Drew some time ago. Tell him I was asking for him...... What would be your pleasure?"

"Yes, hello, Sally. I will remember you to him......, and yes, we will have three mugs of house ale," Philip replied shyly, somewhat surprised she remembered his name. As she left to retrieve the ales, the boys' eyes followed her momentarily, and when she was out of sight, they resumed their conversation

"What do you think, Peter? The taxation is justified, I think," Michael stated directly and without hesitation.

Peter was the gentlest of Philip's friends, as he was when they had attended school together in their youth, perhaps because of the influence of his Anglican minister father, or perhaps it was just the way he was, a soft-spoken gentle person with very refined ways.

"The British have spent a great deal to drive out the French and to help protect the colonies. And without the crown's dollars, churches like your father's, Peter, would not be able to exist. And what would we be without any religion here in this uncivilized part of the world? Don't you agree?" Michael continued.

Peter's sheepish nod was enough for Michael to conclude that Peter agreed. Philip was not so sure. Peter kept his views close to his vest and revealed them so seldom that Philip was never sure of how he felt about anything. Peter had been helping his father teach the youngsters in the region in the church school but did not share his father's interest in the life of a cleric. He was looking forward to becoming an apprentice to his bachelor uncle, his father's brother who was a silver smith in Bennington, Vermont with no heir to whom he could leave his business, save Peter.

"What do you think, Philip?" queried Michael.

"I would tend to agree with you, Michael. And more so, Britain and other countries of Europe have taken hundreds...no, thousands of years, to build the codes of law and behavior to successfully rule a country and its people. No one should think so lightly of this as to want to tear it down because one does not agree entirely with everything the government does. We certainly cannot all agree on everything."

Sally returned with the ales and the conversation halted briefly as all three young men smiled and thanked Sally. Putting the seriousness of the moment aside, the young men shared some memories of their earlier youth as they laughed and drank. As usual Peter said little. Michael talked of someday moving to New York and Philip talked of the forest and the wild.

"I would be on my way to New York to study Law right now if I had my way, offered Michael, but my father says I should wait until the British quell this unrest and things get back to normal. We are the same age, Philip, and you are completely on your own."

"Yes, Michael, but my circumstances are quite different. I am sure my father would treat me in a comparable manner if he were here to do so. I miss my father very much. Be thankful you still have your father to guide you."

"Yes, I am sure you are right. I must believe that for a while longer."

Breathing a sigh, Philip rose to his feet followed by Michael and Peter.

"I'll get this," replied Philip as he headed toward the bar in search of Sally. Michael and Peter exited the tavern and waited for him just outside the entrance. Once outside of the tavern together, all three young men seemed somewhat reluctant to go their separate ways.

"Well, Philip, this is the last we will see each other for a while. In a couple of weeks, I will do what I can as a Loyalist here if I cannot escape to New York, and, if Peter has his way, he will be off to Bennington to apprentice for his uncle," Michael shared with a smile.

Then, in silence for several seconds, Peter nervously stared at the ground, and Philip and Michael looked into each other's eyes, all three men wondering if and when they would see each other again. The three young men were not sure of what to say or do next. After a few seconds of silence, Philip reached out to embrace his friends. Philip mounted his horse, and, as he tugged the reins to one side to turn and head his horse in the direction of the river road, he looked back. Both men standing side by side waved back without any further words, and Philip spurred his horse into a trot in the direction of his farm. These were three young men, each with quite different demeanors, with different dreams on three different paths, but friends forever. Each had no idea when they might meet again.

━━◯◯━━

The American boycott of English imports spread to Boston the following December. At about the same time, General Thomas Gage, commander of English military forces in America, petitioned the New York assembly for legislation requiring the colonists' compliance with the Quartering Act which required colonists to house and supply British troops.

Early in 1766, Benjamin Franklin, as a member of the Assembly of Pennsylvania, traveled to Britain where he addressed the English Parliament and argued for the repeal of the Stamp Act. He warned of a possible revolution in the colonies if the British military enforced the act. After much debate, the Stamp Act was repealed by the parliament and signed by King George III in March. However, almost simultaneously, the English parliament passed the Declaratory Act, declaring that the colonies and plantations were "subordinate unto, and dependent on the imperial crown and Parliament of Great Britain." The news of the Stamp Act's repeal the following month was greeted with great celebrations and the boycott of imported English goods was relaxed.

However, the colonists were still not happy with having to house and feed British troops as required by the Quartering Act. As if invasion of the homes of the colonists by those who opposed foreign rule was not enough, British officers and soldiers became controlling and unruly in pubs and other public places. They would make up and sing songs insulting the colonists, publicly displaying their contempt for the very people forced to host them in their homes and to provide them with food and shelter. The drunker they got, the louder they sang!

A favorite was the song, Yankee Doodle Dandy, which originated on the European continent and was brought to the American continent by the British troops. Although the British soldiers would often add verses created extemporaneously, their favorite and best-known verse was:

Yankee Doodle came to town

Riding on a pony;

He stuck a feather in his cap

And called it macaroni.

Yankee Doodle, keep it up,

Yankee Doodle dandy;

Mind the music and the step,

And with the girls be handy.

"Yankee was a general term of contempt. Doodle referred to a lowly provincial person, while a dandy was a middle-class man meticulously dressed, usually in silk, who affected the fashions and mannerisms of an aristocratic lifestyle in order to gain social status. The macaroni was a type of wig popular in the elite circles of western Europe. So, in other words the song intimated that this country bumpkin comes along on a pony, not a horse, and thinks that merely sticking a feather in his hat would turn him into a suave sophisticate like themselves.

Such public and private invasion into the lives of the colonists served to further incite the actions of patriotic organizations like the Sons of Liberty.

By late summer, there were conflicts in New York City between British soldiers and the colonists often instigated by the Sons of Liberty in opposition to the Quartering Act. That following December, the New York legislature voted to refuse to comply with the act. In response, the English Crown suspended the legislature.

In June of the following year, The English Parliament passed the Townshend Revenue Acts imposing a new series of taxes on the colonists to offset the costs of administering and protecting the American colonies.

The new law taxed, among other things, paper, tea, glass, and paints. In reaction that October, Bostonians again reinstated the boycott of many items imported from England.

Anticipating continued growing unrest with England, Philip Schuyler was commissioned a colonel in the Continental Army to command a new regiment of militia north of Albany. In 1768, Schuyler was also chosen to represent Albany in the colonial assembly. There, in the minority, he advocated strong measures in support of the rights of the colonists. In February, Samuel Adams, as member the of the Massachusetts House of Representatives, wrote and circulated his *Circular Letter* among the colonial assemblies. In it, once again he advocated opposing taxation without representation and called for the united action of the colonies against the British government.

In April, Lord Hillsborough, England's Secretary of State for the Colonies, ordered all colonial assemblies to not endorse the *Circular Letter*. Ignoring the order, by the month's end, the assemblies of New Hampshire, Connecticut and New Jersey endorsed the letter.

The following month, a British warship armed with 50 cannons arrived in Boston harbor. In June, a sloop owned by John Hancock containing imported wine docked in the same harbor was unloaded illegally onto the docks without payment of duties. Customs officials seized Hancock's sloop. Threats of violence from the Bostonians forced customs officials to retreat to an island off the coast of Boston from which they requested intervention by British troops.

In August, Boston merchants boycotted most British goods until the Townshend Acts were repealed. They also convinced merchants in New York to follow suit. Further, in September, Boston residents were urged to arm themselves. The next month, English warships arrived in Boston Harbor followed by two regiments of English infantry to keep order. In March of 1769, merchants in Philadelphia joined the boycott of British goods. During the following January, several men were seriously wounded in a conflict in New York between the Sons of Liberty and forty or so British soldiers. In March, harassment of British soldiers by an angry mob resulted in the soldiers firing their muskets directly into the crowd, killing three men instantly mortally wounding two and injuring six others. Captain Thomas Preston and eight of his men were arrested and charged with murder. To avoid further violence between the colonists and British troops, Samuel Adams met with the Royal Governor of Massachusetts, Thomas Hutchinson, and convinced him that the British troops should vacate the city. Hutchinson agreed and withdrew the troops to the nearby harbor islands.

In April, the British repealed the Townshend Acts, and all duties on imports into the colonies were removed except for tea. The Quartering Act was also not renewed. During the following October, the British soldiers arrested were tried. Captain Preston and six of his men were acquitted, but two other soldiers were found guilty of manslaughter.

The Tea Act of May 10, 1773 imposed a three penny per pound import tax on tea arriving in the colonies. In September, the East India Company shipped 500 pounds of tea to a select group of tea agents. In October, colonists held a mass meeting in Philadelphia opposing the tea tax and forcing the British tea agents to resign their positions. The following month, a town meeting in Boston endorsed the actions taken by the Philadelphia colonists but failed to convince their British tea agents to resign.

Within weeks, three ships bearing tea docked in Boston harbor. Two mass meetings were held during the last days of November in Boston to decide what to do about the tea aboard the ships. The colonists ordered one of the ships to return to England without paying any import duties. The Royal Governor of Massachusetts, Thomas Hutchinson, ordered harbor officials not let the ship sail out of the harbor without the tea taxes being paid. On the night of December 16th, the colonial activists disguised themselves as Mohawk Indians, boarded the ships and dumped all 342 containers of tea into the harbor. The event soon became known as the Boston Tea party.

In March of 1774, English Parliament passed the first of a series of Coercive Acts in response to the rebellious acts in Massachusetts. The Boston Port Bill ordered all commercial shipping in Boston harbor be shut down until the Massachusetts colony paid all taxes owed on the tea dumped in the harbor and had reimbursed the East India Company for their loss.

On May 12ᵗʰ, Bostonians called for a boycott of British imports at a town meeting in response to the Boston Port Bill. General Thomas Gage, as commander of British military forces in the colonies, arrived in Boston with four regiments of British troops and placed Massachusetts under military rule.

On May 20ᵗʰ, the English Parliament enacted the next series of Coercive Acts which virtually ended self-rule by the colonists. Instead, the English Crown and the Royal governor assumed all political power previously exercised by colonists. In June, an updated version of the 1765 Quartering Act was enacted by the English Parliament. It ordered the American colonies to provide housing for British troops in occupied houses, taverns, and unoccupied buildings. In September, Massachusetts Governor Gage seized the colony's arsenal of weapons at Charlestown. During September and through October 26, fifty-six delegates of the First Continental Congress met in Philadelphia. Attendees including Patrick Henry, George Washington, Sam Adams, and John Hancock, declared their opposition to the Coercive Acts and ordered that they were not to be obeyed. Calling for the formation of local militia units, a statement entitled the Declaration and Resolves was adopted. It opposed the Coercive Acts and other measures that undermined self-rule. The representatives asserted their rights to "life, liberty and property." On October 20th, the Congress agreed to a boycott of English imports once again, an embargo of exports to Britain, and discontinuance of the slave trade.

———

The threat of violence grew day by day. However, the hostility did not occur overnight. It was like a slow burning fuse that slowly grew hotter, sometimes sputtered, and then grew hotter again along its way toward the explosive. The fuse now fully in flame was just inches away from detonating the explosive. The quarrel between Britain and the colonies came to a head on April 18, 1775. British General Thomas Gage, Commander in Chief of all British forces in North America, hoped to prevent violence by seizing the weapons and powder stored in Concord, Massachusetts, about twenty miles northwest of Boston. Following orders to accomplish such, British troops departed Boston late in the evening on April 18, 1775 and marched into the town of Lexington around daybreak the next morning.

That night, Paul Revere and William Dawes were sent from Boston to warn colonists of the British plan. Revere reached Lexington about midnight and warned Sam Adams and John Hancock and alerted the Patriot militia called the Minutemen. Waiting to greet them was Captain John Parker who had assembled a small militia company of about 70 men. The flame had reached the explosive! Without an order issued on either side, a shot rang out without anyone sure of who fired. The tense British soldiers reacted impulsively and fired a volley. Seven militiamen were killed, and another mortally wounded. Parker's men fled, while the British soldiers moved on towards Concord.

Arriving at the North Bridge, the British companies of about 220 men in total led by Commanders Francis Smith and Jon Pitcairn were met by a force of around 400 colonial militiamen from the area who had gathered on the high ground across the river overlooking the north bridge. From this vantage point, they could see smoke rising from supplies the British had discovered and burned.

"Will you let them burn the town down?" Lieutenant Joseph Hosmer shouted.

"I haven't a man afraid to go," retorted Captain Isaac Davis as the Minutemen proceeded to advance on the British. The British soldiers opened fire killing both Hosmer and Davis.

"For God's sake, fire!" the Minutemen's Major Buttrick shouted.

The British were forced to retreat across the bridge to take up a defensive position. British troops opened fire again and the Minute Men responded with a volley killing three British soldiers and wounding nine others, with the volley that would come to be known as the shot heard around the world. The British troops retreated back to the town and, feeling vulnerable, decided to return to Boston. Thousands of militiamen attacked the British column from all sides, from behind trees, rocks, and buildings, inflicting heavy casualties on the retreating British regulars.

General Gage ordered Lord Percy to march from Boston with a relief column where they met Pitcairn's men on the eastern outskirts of Lexington. However, as the word spread throughout the surrounding area, the colonial forces grew even greater in number. The British continued to fight in retreat until they could find cover from the British guns in ships anchored in the harbors around Boston. When the fighting ceased, the British had lost 73 men, and many more were wounded. The colonial patriots lost 49 men.

Two months later, on June 17th, 1775, in the Battle of Bunker Hill, the British succeeded in taking Breed Hill, where the battle actually took place, but lost half their force, over a thousand casualties, with the Americans losing but 400 men. The victory was short lived, however, since the colonial rebels reclaimed the hill the following day.

⟶◦◦◦⟵

It was a few days after the Battle of Bunker Hill, on June 25, 1775, as Philip was heading toward the door to exit Pearson's store with a box of supplies, that the door burst open, and Philip's friend, Michael Emerson, appeared. As their eyes met, they both stopped dead in their tracks.

"Oh my God, Philip!" Michael exclaimed.

Philip quickly placed the box on the floor. As he rose, both men broke into wide grins and loud laughter as they embraced.

The stove which heated the store during the winter months sat in the center of the store. To the right and left of the stove, two benches faced each other. At the end of one bench sat a pickle barrel and at the corresponding end of the other a cracker barrel. Occupying the benches were several local colonists deep in conversation. Michael grasped Philip's shoulder, turned, and strode in the direction of the group. He released his grasp, looking over his shoulder as he did so, and gestured to Philip to follow him.

"Come, Philip!" Michael said excitedly.

Philip followed and found a place to stand behind one of the benches where several men were seated. Michael's raised voice attracted some men at the counter, who turned and moved closer. Michael immediately spotted his and Philip's friend, Peter Framingham, seated on a bench listening attentively to the men deep in conversation. Michael quickly moved toward Peter, and with Peter still seated, Michael patted Peter on the shoulder with his left hand, and with it still on his shoulder, shook Peter's hand with his right hand.

"Philip, Peter, everyone, I have some great news. A few days ago, back in Boston, hundreds of Rebels occupied Breed's Hill, but then thousands of British soldiers charged the hill. The battle lasted about 20 minutes and the Rebels ran out of ammunition and retreated. Hopefully, this is the first and last battle we shall see, and we can now all get back to business."

It was obvious that Michael's news was being met with mixed reactions. Those who were Loyalists were in the majority and, like Michael, were also the most vocal, sharing in Michael's exuberance. Those siding with the Rebels frowned and tried to hide angry faces as they stared at the floor or made silent eye contact with each other. Peter Framingham remained silent as usual.

With the men still buzzing amongst themselves, Philip lifted his box of supplies and followed by Michael and Peter, began to head for the door. When they reached the door, the men stepped aside so as not to block the only public access to the store.

"Good Lord, Philip, it's good to be back and to see you again, isn't it Peter?" Michael exclaimed with a broad smile. Peter nodded in agreement. "Still hunting and trapping?"

"Yes, still at it. So glad to see you both. This is a rare opportunity. How have you both been?"

The young men followed two patrons out the door. As they were exiting the store, the men continued to catch up on the paths each of their lives had taken since the last time they had been with each other at the Bemis Tavern so many years ago. They descended the steps and stopped by the hitching rail

"What have you been up to, Michael?" queried Philip.

"Just biding my time helping on the farm for now. I have been in New York studying Law while working odd jobs to sustain myself... seems like forever. Back when I told my father of my plan, it took some time to convince him, but he realized, as well as I, that there was no real opportunity to study law here. He always considered it a noble profession, so he finally gave me his blessing. Although it appears that the British should have things back under control soon, we decided it might be better to come back home for a while until things settle down. I only wish I could help in some way."

"And you, Peter?" Philip asked of his friend as he gently jabbed Peter's shoulder with his fist.

"Spent several years apprenticing with my silversmith uncle in Vermont. Just like Michael's father, my father wanted me back, hoping the relationship between the colonies and Britain will get cleared up. So, since I've been back, I've been helping him however I can, doing lots of reading.....history, philosophy, religion. Even did a little preaching and school teaching. I'm anxious to get back to Bennington though. Was almost finished with my apprenticeship when all this trouble broke out. Will be heading back soon, I hope. My father agrees it's time I made my own way. It's long overdue.

I hope I'll be seeing both of you again before you head out. I need to get back to my place to dress out a deer and tan some pelts, but I'm here about every two weeks either to get supplies or bring in some pelts."

"I look forward to it," Michael replied, patting Philip on the back.

Peter silently reached out and shook Philip's hand. Turning and looking over his shoulder as Philip headed toward the wagon, he acknowledged both men once more, calling their names and pointing in their direction.

"Michael........Peter............'til we meet again my friends."

As he loaded the wagon with his supplies, recalling what he had just heard in the store, he could not help but think about Michael's sense that things would be settling down, but he could not share Michael's confidence, at least not quite yet. All that was happening around him was happening in a world apart from his world, a world in which he had never had any desire to be a part. He recalled that fateful day in the autumn of 1775, when from a hill high above Lake George, he saw the spiral of smoke that signaled the most profound change to ever occur in his life, a life that had been idyllic for ten years as a long-hunter. It was a change that Philip could not have ever anticipated. As he climbed aboard his wagon and nudged his horse in the direction of his little farm, somehow, he felt his life was about to change once again.

CHAPTER 5

The remains of the last two crisscrossed logs tumbled into the glowing embers of the fire, revealing just how long Philip had been speaking. Now only the glowing embers, the stars, and the moon broke the total darkness of the night. Philip had skipped many of the details of his life, but nonetheless, he could not remember ever talking so much to anyone. He was realizing that when he was around this young woman, he had only met a few short hours ago, he was a different person. Philip rose to put more logs on the fire.

"And how about you, Renee? How did your family end up settling here?" he asked as he sat down with his back against the fallen oak log.

"My father found this spot overlooking the lake when he fought in the French and Indian War. He went back to Montreal to get my mother and bring her here."

"Why did he want to leave Montreal?"

"His parents had passed, and he said the only thing he had left in Canada was his father's debts, so he left to escape from them. I was born here, and I know no other place except the honorable General Schuyler's house in Saratoga."

Philip was shocked. This woman perhaps had been geographically close to him during her life, and yet they had passed as ships in the night.

"General Schuyler...Philip Schuyler?"

"Yes, you see, you are not the first Philip in my life," she said as she smiled and tilted her head to one side.

"How did it happen that you knew General Schuyler?"

Renee's mother stirred and made soft hardly audible sounds. Renee crawled to her side and lifted her head.

"Mama, can you take a drink?" she asked, holding a cup of water to her lips. Renee's mother took barely a sip, as she fell back into her bed of pine needles.

Renee crawled back to Philip, leaning against the fallen tree, but sitting closer this time, almost touching his arm.

"My mother met a woman, Mrs. Clark, in the settlement by the lake who worked for the Schuyler's during the summers. My father would be gone much of the time during the summers on his trapping trips. Mrs. Clark asked General Schuyler, but of course he was not a general then, if my mother could also work in his home helping in the kitchen and with other household chores. The general agreed and my mother would bring me along. Mrs. Clark introduced me to English for the first time. Later, when I was old enough to be useful, I worked there also."

"My God, we were so close. We may have even seen each other. I had reason to visit General Schuyler's summer home many times. After serving under him during the war, my father helped to build his Saratoga estate, and my father became a tenant on the farmland on which we lived. After my father died, General Schuyler, out of respect for my father's service under him during the war, transferred ownership of the farm to me and my mother, and after my mother passed, it became mine. I felt that Mr. Schuyler had been too generous, but he insisted. Renee, you loosen my tongue, but we should sleep."

"Yes, I must say I am exhausted."

Exhausted both physically and emotionally, Renee crawled next to her mother, and Philip laid down along the fallen oak. This was the first of many nights they would spend together in this manner.

The next morning, when she awoke, Renee rolled over and looked to where Philip had lain, but he was not there. Her eyes searched the clearing, but he was nowhere to be seen. A pot of water was simmering on the coals. An area approximately ten feet by twenty feet on the opens side of the cabin's fireplace had been cleared of ashes and debris, and in its place rose the beginnings of a lean-to with the top edge resting along the fireplace wall. A rifle shot rang out in the distance from the woods, and Renee's heart seemed to suddenly stop, and then pounded loudly. Her mind returned quickly to the Indians, and she reached for her father's rifle, laying quietly by her mother's side. Within ten minutes, Philip emerged from the woods. His rifle was in his right hand, a dead rabbit dangled from his left

"Dinner," he said, raising the rabbit in the air.

"Your rifle shot scared me to death."

"I'm sorry, I wanted to get an early start. We have much to do." Philip pointed toward the lean-to. "We will not be able to move your mother for some time I am afraid. There is some oatmeal and sugar in my pack, but I am sorry...no milk."

"What, you forgot the milk?" she asked, with the smile that Philip was becoming accustomed to, and which seemed to always lift his spirit, when, indeed, it was Renee's spirit that truly needed lifting.

"Renee, I am sorry that I cannot lift your spirit as you have lifted mine," Philip said, not believing these words were coming from his mouth. What power does this woman have over me? he thought to himself.

"But, Philip, you do lift my spirit. You were sent to me by God, I am sure." Philip blushed and looked at the ground.

"I am not so sure of that, but I am grateful to whatever or whoever it was that brought me here."

Renee touched Philip's hand. Their eyes met and lingered for a moment. No words were spoken. Their eyes spoke for them. Then she dropped her hand and slowly turned to retrieve the oatmeal from his pack. After a breakfast of oatmeal and tea Philip completed the lean-to by cutting saplings, retrieving small fallen trees, and then covering the structure with pines boughs. Renee and Philip then moved the beds of pine needles and their paltry supplies inside the lean-to and finally moved her mother to rest on them, making her as comfortable as possible.

For the next several weeks, Renee tended to her mother while Philip hunted and trapped. He did not venture too far from the clearing, ever mindful of Renee's fathers dispute with the Indians over territorial rights. His thinking was that, since Mr. Merneau had lived and trapped there so long, surely the disputed area was some distance from the immediate surroundings. Even at that, not wanting to attract attention, he used his rifle sparingly, occasionally shooting a pheasant or a turkey and trapping rabbits for food.

In the evenings, Renee would lie next to her mother, embracing her with her head on her mother's shoulder and her arm across her chest. Philip's insight told him that this must be how a small girl embraces her mother, and he felt that Renee was holding onto something and someone she knew she would not have much longer. Philip would sit by the fireplace reading his philosophy books.

"What are the books you read?" Renee asked one night.

"They are philosophy books by men like Plato, Aristotle, Socrates, Locke, ...Descartes."

"I have never seen anyone read a book other than the bible."

"Yes, not many people have books other than the bible, but they were a gift to me as a child, and I truly cherish them."

"I can see that, and I love to watch you read them, but where did you get them?"

"Remember I told you that I would bring money to General Schuyler to pay him 15 percent of what we had received for the crops we had grown on our tenant farm."

"Yes," Renee acknowledged, nodding her head.

"After my father died, my mother brought me to the manor one day on the first of the month, and, while she was working in the kitchen, she sent me to his office in the house with the money to pay him. He was not there, and I was allowed to wait in his office until he returned. I began to read some of the books from his bookshelf, and it was then that, having learned of my father's death, General Schuyler gave the farm to my mother and me. It was also then that he gave these Philosophy books to me. He said they would help me to grow into a wise man."

"And did it work?" she asked with a capricious smile.

Philip returned the smile.

"I certainly hope so. Only time will tell."

Renee's mother slipped alternately in and out of consciousness, only once saying anything loud enough for Philip to hear. Renee would lean down placing her ear close to her mother's mouth, but she often could not understand her utterances.

The only time Philip heard Renee's mother speak loud enough to hear and clearly enough to understand, she spoke but one word as Philip was standing at the entrance of the shelter and Renee was hanging some clothing on an improvised clothesline between two trees some ten feet away.

"Water," she gasped.

"Renee," Philip called, gesturing towards her mother.

Renee hastily walked toward Philip, handing him a piece of the clothing she had washed after rescuing it from the ashes, had subsequently washed, and was about to hang on the clothesline. Renee put a ladle of water to her mother's lips, but she barely had the strength to sip. She laid her mother's head down, and her mother slipped back into an unconscious state. Renee stood and exited the shelter. She walked back to the clothesline and bent over the basket that held a few other pieces of clothing. As she did so, she remembered the piece of clothing she had handed Philip.

"Philip. Please hand me what you have in your hand."

Philip quietly approached her from behind. When he reached her and was standing directly behind her, Renee was not initially aware of his presence. Then suddenly feeling his presence, she turned.

"Oh," she exclaimed, startled by his closeness, and by reflex placed her hand on Philip's chest.

When she realized where her hand was, she moved instinctively to lift it away, but a stronger force told her to leave it there. Returning her hand to his chest, she gazed up at Philip with a look he had never seen before. He thought he knew what the gaze meant but could not be sure. He dropped the piece of clothing on the ground and slowly put his hands around her waist, returning her gaze. He cleared his throat.

"May I kiss you?"

A slight whimsical smile crossed her lips and she whispered, "To ask is not so romantic."

"Yes, but.........but suppose I tried to kiss you, and you pushed me away? I am not prepared to handle that."

"Less prepared for that than if I said no?" she asked, lifting her eyebrows and pursing her lips?

He paused to think. "I don't know, now that you ask, but I guess, at least if you answer, I will know exactly where I stand."

"Oh, you would not know exactly where you stand if I were to turn away?"

"I'm not sure I am astute enough to interpret such a rebuff."

"Oh yes you are, because we...women I mean ...... can turn away in different ways with different meanings. One way says, no, not ever, but another says, not now but maybe someday. And even another says No, not now, not just yet, but soon, so try again."

"You give me greater credit than I deserve." He was silent for a moment, thinking about what he would say next. "I prefer an answer to my question."

"And if I do not choose to answer?" she said with a silly smirk and a twist of her head.

He paused a moment and then slowly leaned forward to kiss her. Renee pulled away, giggling softly. Seeing the look of disappointment on Philip's face, she quickly smiled, while circling his neck with her arms, and leaning upward and forward, she kissed him deeply.

"Now, do you know where you stand?"

"Yes and thank God it is as I had wished."

She giggled, and they separated with both hands interlocked. They backed away looking into each other's eyes for a moment.

"Did you ever read about King Arthur and the Knights of the Round Table?" Philip asked. Somewhat embarrassed, she looked at the ground.

"Philip, I cannot read, but I have heard of the legend. I have not been to school."

"But you speak English. How did you learn to speak it so well?"

"I would say it was a matter of survival. My father suspected often that the fur trading agents in Lake George and Bolton took advantage of him because of his inability to speak English well. As I grew older, I would accompany him, and on such occasions the wife of the agent in Bolton took pity on me and would spend time with me on each visit to help me improve my English, but she never taught me to read."

"No matter. I did not mean to embarrass you. I will teach you. I just wanted to tell you that, when I read the book given to me about King Arthur and his knights, the first woman I ever fell in love with was Lady Guinevere. As I read, I was saddened to think that I would never find such a woman as Lady Guinevere. But now I have found her. Renee, you are my Guinevere!"

She said nothing but raised her right hand to caress his cheek. Then, she turned, picked the piece of clothing from the ground and returned to her work, as Philip watched in admiration.

Renee's mother never did show any signs of improvement, and the periods of consciousness became shorter and less frequent. She developed a fever, and all Renee knew to do was to place cold wet clothes on her forehead. She sat by her side doing such many times for hours each day and into the night. Then, one day, when Philip returned from hunting, he entered the shelter to find Renee holding her mother's head in her lap and crying. She looked up at Philip.

"She is gone," she said simply.

Renee laid her mother's head back and reached out her hand to Philip. Philip grasped her hand to help her to her feet. She buried her head in Philip's chest and continued to sob.

Renee raised her head to look into Philip's eyes. "Do you still miss your mother and father?" she asked.

"Yes," Philip responded.

"I am so glad," she said and kissed him gently on the lips.

Philip and Renee placed her mother next to her father's grave and temporarily covered her with a blanket until they could decide what to do. They knelt beside her together. Philip reached to hold Renee's hand and turned to her. He realized he did not even know her parents' names.

"Renee, I.... I don't even know their names. My life in the woods these past years has left me disrespectful. I am so sorry."

"No, Philip. What is in a name? We are all simply children of God......they are Robert, or Beau, and Joan Merneau, children of God."

"God have mercy on their souls. I do not know any words to say; I am not a religious man, Renee. I do not have an appropriate prayer."

He held her left hand as Renee made the sign of the cross with her right hand and recited the *Our Father* and the *Hail Mary* in French. Philip rose, and with their hands still clasped, he helped Renee to her feet.

"Do you wish to return to Canada?"

"No, I have no one there. I have lived here my whole life."

"Then, you will come to Saratoga with me, but if so............" He hesitated, looked at the ground, and paused for a moment, searching for the words. After a few seconds, he looked up and stared deeply in her eyes. "It would be better if we were married."

"Is that a proposal?" she asked with a wry smile and her head tilted in that teasing way that Philip had come to know so well.

"Yes....I mean No," Philip was embarrassed, and his face became flushed. He looked at the ground once again and he nervously started to move the dirt with his boot back and forth.

"What I mean is I live alone. My house......my parents' house is small. My parents are dead, and I have no place else to offer you. We can't live together if we are not married, and I know it is too soon for you to decide. I...I... I love you very much," he managed to get out, fearing her reaction, which showed on his face.

"So, it is not a proposal? If it is not a proposal, I cannot answer."

There was that silly smirk again. Seeing it relaxed him.

"Yes...yes, okay, it is a proposal then."

She stepped towards him, smiling, and took both of his hands in hers.

"Well, then, you are right. It is too soon," she replied with a serious expression on her face.

Philip's face saddened as his face dropped toward the ground!

"And my answer is............ yes."

He looked down at her, somewhat in disbelief, smiled, or better yet, grinned. Then he looked up at the sky and let out a yell that echoed through the air and would have challenged the best Indian war whoop anyone had ever heard. Renee laughed and then giggled like a young girl. Still grinning, he moved his hands to her waist, and hoisted her into the air. She put her hands on each side of his face. Both smiles faded into a kiss as she wrapped her arms around his neck.

As Philip lowered her to the ground, Renee's smile was replaced by a look of sadness. With the memory of the recent death of both her mother and father always in the back of her mind, she held Philip's hands again, looked up and said, "I wish my mother and father could have met you and given us their blessings."

"As do I, and my parents as well. That would have been a wonderful thing."

"Where will we marry and what will we tell anyone who is bold enough to ask about the suddenness?"

"We can get married by the minister of the church in Saratoga, and we will tell them our parents arranged the marriage long ago if you feel that will give a better appearance."

"I doubt anyone will believe such a story. Your parents are English, mine French. I am sure they would not have approved of you marrying a French Catholic."

"I really don't care if anyone believes it or not. I do not feel a responsibility to tell them anything. So be it. Let them believe what they wish. And I would like to believe my parents would love anyone that I loved."

"Perhaps it might be better if we were already married when we arrive in Saratoga. We can be married by the priest at the Catholic Church in the settlement at the south end of Lac du Saint Sacrement. Do you mind marrying in a Roman Catholic Church?"

The lake was renamed Lake George after the French and Indian War, but Renee preferred to still call it the name given it by the French missionary, Father Isaac Jogues in 1646 before the English changed the name.

"I think that it might be better to marry before we reach Saratoga as well, and I prefer to marry in the church of your choice."

"Thank you, Philip. Then we shall marry in the Catholic church by the lake, and I would like to have a proper service for my mother and father also. Then they can be laid to rest in the little cemetery behind the church."

"So, shall it be," replied Philip as he wrapped her in his arms and kissed her.

———ᴍᴍᴜᴜᴍᴍ———

Lake George, located about thirty miles north of Saratoga, is thirty-two miles long, three miles wide at its widest, and nearly 200 feet deep at its deepest. The first non-Native discoverer of the lake was either Samuel de Champlain the early 1600's explorer or Father Isaac Jogues, the French missionary who gave the lake its French name, Lac du Sacrament (Lake of the Blessed Sacrament) in the 1640's.

When the French and Indian War broke out over the French's attempted expansion into British Colonial territory, the region became important to secure. When British General Edward Braddock traveled north to take on the French, he renamed the lake, Lake George in honor of the British king. In 1755, the British won the Battle of Lake George. Fort William Henry was built by the British in that same year but was burned to the ground in 1757 after being attacked by the French. After the second battle, the British agreed to surrender and were allowed to retreat south to Fort Edward. However, the Indians fighting on the side of the British were not pleased and massacred as many as 1,500 unarmed soldiers, civilians, women, and children. The French officers who risked their lives trying to stop the natives returned to the fort and burned it to the ground.

———ᴍᴍᴜᴜᴍᴍ———

The open practice of the Catholic religion was forbidden in the New York colony, so after Philip and Renee entered the little inconspicuous Catholic chapel, unidentified as such, the door was locked from the inside and a guard was stationed outside the door to warn of any intruders. After a Roman Catholic burial mass, followed by a mass where the pastor administered the Catholic sacrament of Holy Matrimony, Renee's parents were interred behind the little chapel. Soldat laid down between the two graves until Philip was able to convince him to follow him and Renee back to the site of the burned-out cabin. When the newlyweds reached the site, Philip built a travois to be pulled by his horse on which he and Renee tied down the few items rescued from the fire. Philip lifted Renee atop his horse and led the horse to the head of the trail toward the lake. Once more Philip had to convince Soldat to leave his master behind and to reluctantly follow him and Renee. Renee looked over her shoulder to view one last time the once beautiful little clearing overlooking the lake, where now only the shelter stood leaning against the cabin chimney. This had been the place of her birth and the only home she had ever known. A few small tears trickled down her cheeks. She raised her chin as she turned to face the trail and her unknown life ahead while wiping the tears from her eyes. Soldat followed behind reluctantly, somehow as if he was not able at this point to determine where the only master he ever knew really was.

———————

As Philip and Renee guided the horse up the road to the little farmhouse Philip and his parents had called home, he noticed for the first time how overgrown everything was. The grass grew high right up to the house and barn, and the fields, once rich with oats and corn were now covered in weeds. There was a well-worn path from the road to the barn where Drew still performed his smithing and ironworking, but no longer was there a distinct path from the house to the barn or to the stream behind the house. For the first time since his mother's death, Philip remembered how neat and orderly the little farm had always looked when he was a child. Opening the door to the house and staring in, he had the same reaction to the cluttered and dusty room that the sunlight streaming through the grimy windows revealed. Studying Renee's face as she looked about the room, he suddenly was very embarrassed.

"It doesn't look like much now, but when my mother and father were alive, it was a nice home. I have not spent much time here since they both passed. I'm sorry I could not bring you home to something better."

"Philip, it looks like paradise to me. You must look past the dust and the weeds. You must see it how you remember it, and how can be once again... Don't worry, it will look like home, our home ...soon."

Philip looked out a window to determine if Drew was there. He could see his horse tethered to the railing by the barn. He escorted Renee to the barn where he introduced Drew to her. To say that Drew was shocked to learn of their marriage is an understatement, but he was happy for his adopted little brother. When the full story was revealed, including the part where perhaps they might tell Sam Pearson that their marriage was arranged, he was very understanding even though he didn't necessarily support it. Before speaking, he embraced both of them enthusiastically.

"Philip, I don't know how to advise you regarding your creating a story about how your marriage came about. It certainly does not sound like you, or something you would ever feel necessary to do. Renee, I think you have made an excellent choice in Philip, and since I know Philip so well, I think better than anyone on this earth, if he has chosen you, you must be a remarkable woman indeed." Drew paused, clasped his hands, and then added, "You have shared your good news with me.... Now I have some news to share with you. I think this is the time to tell you that I have built a barn behind my cabin to where I will move my smithing and iron-working endeavors."

"Drew, you know that is not necessary. You are well established here and need not move. And you know my father would have felt the same way, so please stay," implored Philip.

"Philip, I appreciate you saying that it is not necessary for me to move. And because my barn is already built, you know this obviously has nothing to do with your marriage, although now it is an additional reason because you newlyweds certainly deserve your privacy. The decision was based on other factors."

"And so, these other factors are...?"

"As you are aware, there have been battles between the colonists that prefer independent rule and the British in both the northeastern and southern colonies already, and there are now rumors that there will be an invasion by the British from Canada with the goal of reaching Albany.

Since Mr. Schuyler is now a General in the Continental Army and has been placed in command of the Northern Division, Philip, he has asked me to enlist in the militia as a blacksmith for the Continental Army, and I have agreed. So far, we have avoided conflict, but one cannot reach Albany from Canada without going through Saratoga. If this is true, I doubt we will be able to avoid the conflict much longer. I know your feelings about war and that you wish to remain neutral, but remember, neutrality favors the aggressor. So, I told General Schuyler I would enlist in the militia and serve as a blacksmith. I would not want soldiers from either side coming to your barn to have their horses re-shoed."

"Thank you, Drew. That barn has been a blacksmith shop my whole life, and I always considered you smithing in it a tribute to my father and a compliment to you because he chose you to carry on his worthy profession. I would have a different attitude if I were alone, but now that Renee is here and we cannot be sure of what fate has in store for us in the near future, I support your decision, and I understand your other decision as well, about the militia I mean. I guess I even envy you in that you now have peace of mind in that regard and are not tortured as I am."

As Drew and Philip embraced, Philip thought about how Drew had mentored and guided him so many times after his father's death but realized this was a decision that he now had to make alone.

———

The new couple settled in and began going about restoring the house and farm to what it had been when Philip's parents were alive. One morning, after about a week or so, Soldat was nowhere to be found. "I believe I know where he is, Philip declared. He remembers where your father is and has returned to his grave to be with him. I am sure of it! I have heard of this happening before when an animal becomes so attached to his master. If you agree, I shall return to the lake to see if I can convince him to come back with me."

Renee nodded approval, and, after breakfast and kissing his wife farewell, Philip mounted his horse and made his way the thirty plus miles to find Soldat lying beside Robert Merneau's grave behind the little

Catholic church by the lake. Philip fed Soldat, who had not eaten in some time and patted him gently while speaking softly in an attempt to win him over as his new master. Philip was able to convince the animal to follow him once more to Saratoga.

Soldat stayed with his new family, and Renee was right. Her vision came to pass in a few short weeks. The little farm began to look like home. Philip acquired a plow horse and a cow. The farm fields were tilled before Thanksgiving and made ready for spring planting. Philip scythed the brush growing about the house and barn to a well-trimmed height. The inside of the house with bright gingham curtains on the windows, the floor swept clean, the furniture dusted and oiled, and fresh clean bedding revealed a woman's touch for the first time since Philip's mother had died. The smell of freshly cooked bread and the cinnamon aroma of just baked apple pie lingered in the air. Philip went on trapping and hunting trips much less often now, and for shorter periods of time, only a day or two. However, his trips to the Pearson's store became more frequent to get supplies that Renee needed. Of course, after the first trip to store, once the Pearsons became aware of Philip and Renee's marriage, the news traveled throughout the region like wildfire. Philip was comforted by the fact that Soldat provided some degree of protection for Renee when he had to be away even if it was to simply warn her of oncoming strangers. He had also taught Renee how to handle a rifle.

Many of the colonists in New York celebrated Thanksgiving in November, and in 1775, soon after, in Saratoga, the winter snows came. The following December and January were exceptionally snowy. Philip had contrived some runners for the wagon so it could be used as a makeshift sleigh during the winter season. On the last day of January 1776, an unusual warm spell occurred, and on a bright sunny day, Philip hitched the horse to the sleigh for a trip to Pearson's store to get some necessary supplies. Philip had heated some bricks by the fire to warm his bride's feet. Renee appeared at the doorway with a blanket under her arm. All was ready, and Philip hoisted Renee up into the sleigh. This would be Renee's coming-out introduction to the Pearsons, and this was the part of the trip that Philip did not especially relish.

"I think you will like Martha, Renee. She is like a little sister to me. Mr. Pearson? Well, that's another story. I'm not too sure about him, but I am sure you will win him over with your charm."

"I'm ready for Mr. Pearson. I am sure we will have more difficult challenges in our marriage than Mr. Pearson," she answered as she smiled and leaned towards Philip and kissed him on the cheek.

Renee was somewhat apprehensive, but being a high spirited, independent woman, she settled into her seat with a sigh. The short ride up the river road to the Pearsons was quite pleasant with the bright sun reflecting off the river flickering through the bare tree branches.

Martha was sweeping the front porch of the store and welcomed Philip and Renee with a smile and a wave. Philip helped Renee down from the sleigh, and, after adjusting her full-length skirt, Renee was the first to ascend the wooden steps to the store's porch. As she reached the top step, Martha, smiling, reached out her hand to take Renee's and was the first to speak. If Martha harbored any jealousy or resentment toward this woman who had married the man she had dreamt of marrying since she was a child, it did not manifest itself in the slightest way.

"Welcome, Mrs. Eames, I am so happy to meet you and so happy that you found our Philip and were able to keep him out of the forest long enough to get him to the altar."

The women embraced, and Renee replied, "Martha, I am so happy to finally meet you. Philip speaks fondly of you often. You have become an important part of his life."

Philip, Renee, and Martha made their way into the store, and after unbundling themselves from their winter outerwear, they huddled around the stove to warm their hands.

"I'll put some water on the stove, and by the time I take your order, the water should be ready for tea," Martha said over her shoulder as she walked toward the stove at the back of the store.

She set some teacups and pastry dishes out on a table at the rear of the store, nestled among some barrels of staples. Then she went behind the counter, tying on an apron as she walked, to take Philip and Renee's order. As Renee and Martha were looking at a bolt of cloth which Martha had spread on the counter to be used by Renee for a dress, Martha's father entered the store from the rear door.

"Father, come and meet Renee, Philip's new bride."

Sam Pearson approached without a smile.

"How do you do, Mrs. Eames. Welcome to Saratoga. I trust your home here will be to your liking," Sam Pearson replied as he nodded a hello towards Philip.

Somewhat prepared by Philip for Sam Pearson's cold demeanor, Renee smiled and offered her thank you for the welcome with her usual smile.

"I am very happy just to be here. And I appreciate the warm welcome from Martha and yourself. Martha has already made me feel at home and Philip has started to put the farm back in order."

One might have thought that Sam Pearson's cool demeanor was due to Renee's ending his dream of Martha marrying Philip and taking over his business someday, but Philip knew that it was just Pearson's way. Pearson went behind the counter, bent over and retrieved a month-old newspaper from New York City, laying it on the counter in front of Philip

"Smythe and Jamieson brought this newspaper back on their last trip. Things seem to be heating up quite a bit with the British. It's getting pretty serious, Philip. I hope they clear this up quickly so we can get back to business as usual."

As the ladies talked and laughed and went about the business of filling the order, Philip took the paper to the table which Martha had set at the back of the store, followed by Pearson. Both men sat down at the table, and Philip began to read, as Sam Pearson looked on.

"I am not pleased to see what is happening, sir. I have lost touch over the past several years, but now that I am married and hope to have a family and build a future, this news is disheartening. It would be a shame to tear down what has taken 150 years to build. Now that the French are no longer a threat, and the colonies are all under the crown, we should all move forward not backward."

The ladies joined the two men and Martha served tea and some fresh baked apple pie. After about an hour's visit, two customers arrived, and when the Pearson's rose to serve them, Philip and Renee rose and made their way to the door. The goodbyes were short as dictated by the Pearson's need to attend to some customers who had just arrived. The ladies hugged and promised to meet again soon at a time during a day when they would not be interrupted. And what had transpired that day between them was all it took for the two women to begin to become close friends. Philip shook Mr. Pearson's hand, and the couple made their way out the door to the landing and down the steps to load the sleigh with their provisions. Once loaded, the newlyweds climbed aboard, and with a final wave they were on their way.

As the horse and wagon made its way down the river road to the small farm, Philip spoke first.

"Well, what do you think of the Pearsons?"

"Martha is such a beautiful person. I can see why you love her."

"I didn't say I loved her."

"You said she was like a sister to you. So, of course you love her. It's quite alright, Philip. I think I could come to love her also."

"And Mr. Pearson," if I dare to ask?

"I think he is a very lonely man. He is not so much different than my own father. It was my mother that made my father smile. If Martha is at all like her mother, I am sure her mother made Mr. Pearson smile."

Then, with a sudden change of subject, Renee queried, "Philip do you have any negative feelings towards the French? I am French, you know?" she added with a wry smile, tilting her head to one side.

"Why do you ask? I did marry a French girl, you know," Philip replied, imitating Renee's smile, phrasing and tone.

"It was just something you said at tea with the Pearson's about being rid of the French."

"I am not sure I said it just that way. In any event, what I meant was that the colonies are now all under British rule, and that rule is no longer threatened by the French government. But, in direct answer to your question, no, I have no negative feelings toward the French people. And in fact, I have very strong feelings toward one particular French girl, with whom I hope to spend the rest of my days. Although, I might add it would not matter if this girl were any other nationality or religion, I would still love her as I do."

Renee put both hands on Philip's right arm, and Philip leaned towards her. They kissed briefly, but long enough such that the sleigh hit an icy spot in the center of the road, and Philip had to react quickly to regain the wagon's stability and regain its track down the center of what was simply a very wide snow covered normally dirt path known as the river road. Once Philip regained control of the wagon, he spoke again for the last time before turning up the winding drive to the little farm.

"I really do not have much interest in, nor do I wish to get involved much in politics, my love. I talk about it with Mr. Pearson or others to be sociable. As far as France and the colonies are concerned, political alignments are quite fickle, based almost entirely on the self-interests of the governments of a country at any particular time. Yesterday's enemy may become tomorrow's ally."

It seemed that Philip did not know how prophetic his comment was for the colonies. But then again, perhaps he did.

CHAPTER 6

The winter was long and cold with an over one-hundred-inch snowfall accumulation, quite typical of upstate New York. However, Philip's contrived snow runners for the wagon provided the ability to get out of the house on milder days, which occurred in mid-February, for a ride to counteract cabin fever, or for a trip to Pearson's store. Being closed in for such extended periods exacerbated the sadness Renee experienced from time to time, still grieving the loss of her parents. Occasionally Philip would find her silently but tearfully gazing out of the window for short periods of time. Philip left her to her thoughts during such times, but when he felt such a period had gone on too long, he would approach her from behind and put his arms around her waist. Then he would kiss her on the neck or nibble on her ear, and she would always wipe her eyes, turn, smile, and kiss Philip on the lips without either of them saying a word. She did not want to be a burden to her new husband, but, having lost his parents as well, he understood her emotions during such times.

Well into winter, Philip and Renee were snowbound often for several days or weeks, many times with subzero temperatures outside. When their meat supply was diminished and the weather permitted, Philip would be pressed into a hunting trip to replenish it. Martha would sometimes stay with Renee during these times if the river road was passable. Otherwise, the winter was spent mostly indoors close to the fire, giving the young couple an opportunity to get to know each other better. Sometime in mid-January Renee had become pregnant, and once her brief period of morning sickness had passed, Philip was able to teach Renee to read from the same children's books from which he had learned, as well as how to write and to improve her arithmetic skills.

Snow remained on the ground well into March and even into April in areas that saw little or no sun. When he could get through the snow, Philip would take the sleigh to the Pearson's store to get supplies and hear the latest news from New York and Boston by way of Albany. On one such trip early in April Philip was finally able to use the wagon for the first time, and upon his return, Renee met him at the door to tell him that one of General Schuyler's help had left just a few minutes earlier and had requested that Philip meet the general at his Saratoga home as soon as possible. This was highly unusual in that during the winter only a small number of house and kitchen help were in residence, and the general usually did not arrive to get things ready for the New Year until after the snow had pretty much cleared for good. Apparently, General Schuyler, along with his wife Catherine, and their daughters, Betsy and Peggy, had arrived at the summer home the previous week and stayed a few days to ready the house for the arrival of guests early in April.

After warming himself, he bundled himself up again and rode to the Schuyler's home to see what it was the general was requesting of him. The meeting was friendly and brief since the general was looking for a quick response. Philip excused himself for not giving an immediate response, asking for an opportunity to speak with Renee before agreeing to the assignment. Without saying it, both men knew that the answer would surely be positive, but that Renee deserved the respect of being informed of the essence of the request, even if not part of the decision.

Upon his return home, Philip entered the little farmhouse, stomped the snow and mud from his feet, and after removing his coat and mittens, went directly to the fire to stoke it and to warm his hands once again. As he rubbed his hands together over the fire, he shared what he had learned with Renee.

"Well, my dear, General Schuyler is here already."

"Mon Deux, what brings him to Saratoga so early?"

"Apparently, he is bringing house guests up from Albany next week."

"What is the occasion?"

"The general didn't say, and no one at the house seems to be quite sure," he replied as he turned to face her and placed his hands on her waist. "General Schuyler is looking for someone to retrieve his guests and transport them from Albany to Saratoga. Morrison, his regular driver, has not come in from his winter quarters yet. He asked if I would mind traveling to Albany in the morning and bringing them back. You would stay at the Schuyler house in the quarters you occupied with your mother years ago. It will provide us with a little extra income to start the year, so I would like to agree to make the trip. Do you approve?" he asked as he returned to stoking the fire.

What Philip could not tell Renee was that this trip was part of a mission by envoys of the Second Continental Congress. The group, led by Dr. Benjamin Franklin, was made up of five men of quite different backgrounds.

"Of course, Philip, but will not the roads be impassible at some points so early in the season?"

Philip put a log on the fire and stoked it.

"One would think so, but the general, his wife, and children made it here a few weeks ago to ready the house for their guests with their Albany driver and the Albany driver returned to Albany the next day. If a driver from the city can make it to Saratoga and back, surely it can be no challenge for an accomplished woodsman," he replied as he turned his head toward Renee and smiled.

Renee smiled back and nodded her head with a facial expression that said, "well am I not a special one!"

"We will have to leave early in the morning if I am to make it to Albany in one day. The general and I agreed we would leave by five o'clock in the morning."

Philip returned to the Schuyler house to report to the general that he was up to the task and then returned home promptly. That evening

Philip and Renee put the things together they would need for Philip's trip and Renee's stay at the Schuyler home. Under cover of darkness the couple left for the Schuyler house, and by five o'clock the next morning, Renee was settled in. Philip kissed Renee goodbye and she escorted him to the door to find the general already waiting for him in the wagon. As Philip climbed aboard the wagon to depart, Philip turned in Renee's direction, kissed his fingers, then extending his open palm toward her and pursing his lips, blew another kiss in her direction.

The carriage had three rows of padded seats behind the driver's seat with padded backs as well. Covered by a flat roof, for the most part, it was an open affair, and Renee's remarks regarding the roads were quite on target. They were treacherous, deeply rutted with trees fallen by the weight of the snow over the winter often partly blocking the way. Crossing the Mohawk and the tributaries of the Hudson twice by ferry near Van Schaik Island offered brief respites. Luckily, as Philip approached Albany, many of the muddy sections of the road were lined with planks. Starting out before dawn, Philip was able to reach the Schuyler's main house in Albany shortly after dusk and spent the night in the servant's quarters.

The following morning, General Schuyler and the five men climbed aboard for the trip to Saratoga. Accompanying Dr. Franklin was a Catholic priest, a Prussian officer, and two other men. Since General Schuyler only introduced the men to him briefly but was not forthcoming about the purpose of the trip, Philip inferred that these five men were apparently on a secret mission. Philip could not conclusively surmise the intent of the trip but was almost certain from whom some of his passengers were, that it most likely had something to do with gaining French support for the colonial position regarding the growing dispute between the crown and the colonies. He could find no other reason for such a contingent to include both the colonies' foremost diplomat in the person of Dr. Benjamin Franklin as well as a Jesuit priest. Canada was predominantly Catholic, and it seemed logical that the Congress would feel that the presence of a Catholic priest would aid in establishing rapport with the Canadians since it was generally known that Catholics were permitted to openly practice in only two colonies, Maryland and Pennsylvania. The only thing that puzzled Philip and did not fit in with his guess at what the trip was about was the inclusion of the Prussian officer. He was introduced to the man, but since he heard his name only once and did not remember it, he hoped he could avoid the embarrassment of ever having to repeat it.

⟶◦⟅⟆◦⟵

Once the British victors in the French and Indian War came to realize that although Canada, or Quebec as it was known, was now part of the British Empire, it would always be French and that the Catholic faith would always be the dominant religion. The Quebec Act allowing Catholics to practice their faith as well as hold public office in Canada had been passed in 1774.

The majority of the members of Congress felt the necessity of foreign alliances in the effort to attain self-rule and independence from Britain. Discussions with France through secret agents yielded little support because France held little confidence that the American colonies would have success in a war with the most powerful military force on earth.

Hoping to gain a foothold in Canada and win the support of the Canadians in the Patriots' cause against Britain, the Congress had authorized an attack on Montreal under General Richard Montgomery in the Fall of 1775. The British held Fort St. Jean's under Major Charles Preston surrendered to the American patriots on November 3rd, fearful of the hardship the town's civilians would face during a winter under siege. With the fortification in Patriot hands and British General Carleton's defenses depleted by previous conflicts, Montgomery's forces entered Montreal without a shot being fired on November 13th. Soon after gaining this foothold in Canada, Congress decided to advance further into Canada with an attack on Quebec City 160 miles to the north of Montreal.

Early in December, forces under General Montgomery and General Benedict Arnold joined to become one force led by Arnold, whose men had made a grueling journey through the wilderness of northern New England. Last minute reinforcements arrived from England to bolster the city's defenses before the colonial attacking force arrived. Montgomery made the attack in a blinding snowstorm hoping to conceal his army's movements. His forces were to converge in the lower city and to then scale the walls protecting the upper city. Montgomery was killed by cannon fire early in the battle and his troops forced to turn back. Arnold's force was able to penetrate further into the lower city, but Arnold was injured in the leg early in the attack. His contingent became trapped in the lower city and was forced to surrender. Arnold and the Americans maintained a fruitless blockade of the city until British reinforcements arrived forcing the American forces to retreat to Montreal on December 31st.

After this devastating defeat in the battle for Quebec, Congress decided that they should take advantage of the American patriot's control of Montreal as perhaps their last chance to convince the Canadians to enter the conflict with Britain on the side of the American colonies.

Hoping to gain support of the Canadians, on February 15, 1776, Congress created a diplomatic commission consisting of Benjamin Franklin, Samuel Chase, like Franklin, a member of Congress from Maryland, and Charles Carroll. Father John Carroll, cousin of Charles Carroll accompanied the commissioners to interact with the Canadian religious authorities. Charles Carroll, another Marylander, a devout Catholic from one of the two states that allowed the practice of the Catholic faith, was to show that Protestants and Catholics could live together harmoniously. He was also a good friend of the colonial northern commander, General Philip Schuyler. Additionally, the personally wealthy Charles Carroll was fluent in the French language, which would hopefully impress the Canadians. He could also act as an interpreter for the other commissioners as well.

After deliberating for a month, Congress formally charged the Commission with the goal of convincing the Canadian people to join the colonies in separating from Britain and, in so doing, would become the fourteenth American colony. With this obviously came the advantage of mutual defense. They were to also be granted free and undisturbed exercise of their religion. Possession and enjoyment of their estates would be granted, as well, along with the establishment of a free press and the right to enact laws governing their colony and representation in Congress. In addition, the Congress was offering four officer commissions, to be selected by the new colony. The commissioned officers were to form and lead four new regiments by enlisting willing volunteers from among the Canadian people.

———⚬⚬⚬———

Philip's return trip from Albany back to Saratoga with his passengers the next day was equally as treacherous as the previous day's trip. The bumpy ride, with a great deal of noise generated by the jostling of the wagon and the wind unblocked by trees still unadorned with leaves, did not allow for much conversation amongst Philip's passengers. What conversation Philip could overhear was quite lighthearted and revealed no additional information relative to the purpose of the forthcoming mission.

Arriving late in the afternoon, after delivering his passengers to the Schuyler's country home, Philip and Renee returned to their little farm where Renee prepared a much-appreciated home cooked meal of venison and potatoes with apple pie for dessert. The next day Philip began to prepare the little farm for the oncoming planting season while waiting for a message from the general that the commissioners had returned from their mission and were ready to be transported back to Albany.

As might be expected, Philip Schuyler was the perfect host and took his guests on a tour of his estate, including his farmlands as well as the mills for grain, lumber, hemp, and flax. The weather turned colder and the commissioners' trip to Lake George where they would head by water up Lake Champlain and on to Canada was delayed for four days. On the fifth day, Schuyler provided for their overland trip to Lake George with his recently arrived regular spring and summer driver where they boarded a bateau. Five days later, on April 29th, after enduring the cruelties of a trip in an open watercraft during winter conditions that took them through wilderness, deep snow, and over poor roads, as well as sleeping in the bateau or in makeshift shelters on shore at night, the commissioners arrived in Canada. Franklin's body suffered greatly from the hardships, manifesting itself with his suffering with boils, gout, and dizziness. On more than one occasion, he felt he may not live to complete the mission. "I begin to apprehend that I have undertaken a fatigue that at my time of life may prove too much for me, so I sit down to write to a few friends by way of farewell," he wrote to his friend Josiah Quincy.

Once arriving in Canada where they were transported to Montreal by carriage, Brigadier General Benedict Arnold, who had commanded the Patriot forces since the capture of Montreal several months earlier, arranged for a cannon salute from the city's citadel and a grand party and feast to celebrate their arrival.

The party was held in the Chateau Ramezay, the opulent residence built at the start of the 18th century by the governor for which it was named in the style of the castles in his native Normandy. The high stone building had a series of dormers and a copper roof. Each room was elegantly decorated and the Nantes Salon, a hall for exhibiting works of art, had walls of elaborately carved hardwood panels designed by a French architect. It overlooked the Rue Notre-Dame and featured beautiful formal gardens on one side and to the rear.

The orchestra played both English and French arrangements as the guests comprised of governmental officials, local Canadian families, and members of Canadian society, entered the hall. The women wore beautiful flowing gowns with empire waists which enhanced and exposed much of their breasts and each with fashionable elaborately styled powdered hair. Many of the families were accompanied by single female family members of various ages, perhaps in the hopes of meeting one of the unaccompanied men who might be members of the landed gentry.

The Carroll cousins, Father John and Charles, wandered across the room to speak with Father Peter R. Floquet and two other Catholic priests identifiable by their white clerical collars, where Charles acted as French interpreter for John. Franklin and Chase stood to one side with Arnold who was pointing out with whom it would be advantageous to speak and where Franklin's diplomatic acumen might do the most good.

"If Charles returns, General, you shall introduce us. I fear my French is not adequate without Charles to facilitate the conversation. If he does not return in a timely fashion, we shall fetch him after giving him adequate time to gain favor with the clergy," suggested Franklin.

"Yes," agreed Chase. Then, with a chuckle, he added, "In the meantime, I shall enjoy the visual pleasure of admiring these beautiful young ladies while lamenting my age and my pledged-fidelity to my wife,"

"My dear friend, how can a man of your age not be aware that your financial status will far outweigh age and countenance with most of these young ladies so long as you have been physically endowed with what it takes to make them smile the next morning after what we might call a romantic evening," Franklin replied with a wry smile as two of the men grinned, fully aware that Benjamin Franklin's reputation with the ladies preceded him. Arnold, although he tried, could not restrain himself from laughing aloud.

Although the commissioners deemed the formal reception a success, their reception was not as impactful on the general populace. Payment for supplies and assistance previously provided to American forces by the Canadians was offered by Franklin using relatively useless Continental dollars. The absence of hard currency to pay for such led to the belief by the Canadians that Congress was bankrupt. For this reason, the Canadians were not prepared to honor Continental currency as payment for future services. The commissioners wrote to Congress requesting twenty thousand pounds to pay off existing debts and to support the war effort. In their request, Franklin noted that it would be impossible to convince the Canadians to join the American efforts against the British without it.

Father John Carroll felt he had made some progress with Father Floquet the night before at the welcoming party and the next day as well. In hopes of further ingratiating the good father, the Patriots returned to him his Montreal home which had previously been used for military use. However, the final decision regarding the support of the Catholic Church was not his. All other Catholic priests followed the orders of the Bishop of Quebec, Monseigneur Briand, and refused contact with Father Carroll. The Monseigneur felt that the British Quebec Act guaranteed the Canadians religious freedom as well as their legal customs, whereas the patriots could only promise as much, but could not guarantee it. In addition, the Canadians were not impressed with the lack of commitment of the many disheartened soldiers who had left the Patriot struggle after the Battle of Montreal and returned home at the conclusion of their enlistment.

The failure of the commissioner's mission with the French, right here on the North American continent, began to raise doubts with Benjamin Franklin. America's leading diplomat questioned that the Patriots could ever win the support of the country of France, thousands of miles away on the European continent without demonstrating something very positive in the campaign.

Without gaining the support the Continental Congress sought from Canada, Franklin felt he had one last task to which he must attend. If the commissioners could not gain support from the Canadians, hopefully he could at least get agreement from the Indians that they would not support the British. The Seven Nations of Canada, the same Indian tribes from the Saint Lawrence River that had fought on the side of the French in the French and Indian War were returning home from a council with the Six Nations of the New York and Great Lakes Region. Coincidentally, the purpose of the council was to discuss just that: whether the Native Americans would remain neutral in a war between the colonies and the British. This effort was an apparent failure in that the Indians reported to Franklin that no decision had been made in this regard by the council. From this Franklin could only conclude that the Indians were biding their time until they could be more assured of who would prevail in such a conflict. They were obviously looking for an agreement with the victor that they would be granted unchallenged land rights to the area of the continent west of the thirteen colonies in trade for their alliance.

Adding to these rather negative results, the planned 8,000 troops in Canada had been reduced to about 3,000. In addition to the soldiers leaving at the conclusion of their enlistment, smallpox had further reduced the numbers. With these numbers, the Patriot positions could not be defended from the reported large numbers of British reinforcements expected to arrive. In fact, the Canadians could reach the point where they viewed the Patriots as the invading and occupying force and might join the British in their efforts against the American colonies. In light of this, the commissioners recommended to the Congress that the Continental Army withdraw to Fort Ticonderoga at the southern tip of Lake Champlain. With the lack of success in their mission and

Franklin's failing health, he and Father Carroll left on May 11ᵗʰ to return to Philadelphia, leaving the other commissioners behind.

The only positive gain for Benjamin Franklin was his acquisition of a soft marten fur hat to protect his bald head from the cold and wind of Canada and northern New York on the trip back.

—◁◁◁◁◁∿◁◁◁◁◁—

The message to return three of the commissioners from Saratoga to Albany came on May 20th[th]. Charles Carroll and Samuel Chase had left Montreal on May 16ᵗʰ, and joining General Schuyler at Fort Ticonderoga, the three men traveled from there to the Schuyler home in Saratoga. Philip was notified that he would have only three passengers to return from Saratoga to Albany, and that the other two commissioners had returned several days earlier by a different route.

Now that the snows had melted, and the drying sun made the roads more easily passable, the trip to return the beleaguered commissioners was much more bearable, and Philip was able to deliver his passengers to Albany and return to Saratoga very expeditiously. What Philip overheard of the conversation between the two men still revealed little about the mission. However, what he did hear indicated that both men were very disappointed by the results of their efforts, and that basically the mission had resulted in failure. Along the way he also heard enough from the conversation to reach the conclusion that the commissioners felt that the colonies had to be on the alert for a possible attack by the British from the north, and ironically, with the Canadians possibly joining them as British, not American patriot allies.

By mid-May, spring finally brought a rebirth to every living thing around Philip and Renee, and with it came a rekindled spirit with hopes and prospects for their future. The trees burst into fullness with buds and then leaves. The wildflowers bloomed in the forests, fields, and beside the riverbanks. Lakes and streams sparkled in the sun's light as the sun rose higher and higher in the sky each day. The rivers, creeks, and streams rushed hurriedly along their paths, gurgling over rocks and splashing against the banks with excitement. Along with the promises of spring, the anticipation of their first child added to the euphoria of the season.

—◆◆◆◆◆—

Philip plowed and sowed the fields of the little farm, and he and Renee knew a happiness that they could only hope would remain with them and sustain them for the rest of their lives. The young couple was so consumed with their lives together that, like the years Philip had spent in the forest as a long-hunter, days and weeks went by with hardly a thought being paid to the political struggles between the colonies and the mother country. Spring passed into summer. The crops were good and attending to the tasks at hand commanded most of Philip's attention.

However, as the year wore on, trips to the Pearson's store became increasingly troubling to Philip as more and more of the discussions around the cracker barrel included attempts by many of the regulars to draw him into taking a position on one side or the other. His only recourse seemed to be to excuse himself, declaring a need to attend to something on his farm, or to escape into the forest on a trapping excursion.

Philip could not deny that these were only temporary solutions to his problem. It was becoming apparent that the crown and parliament were increasingly dominating and controlling every part of colonial life. The economy of the colonies was suffering as well as the rights of its citizens being violated. In light of these developments, how could he justify his loyalty to the king and British rule and at the same time preserve the life he had grown to love here in the colonies without taking sides. All he wished was to be left alone to his life on his farm with his wife who was expecting the birth of their first child very soon. His desires, of course, also included the occasional trapping and hunting trips into the forest for pelts to trade and to hunt venison, fowl, fish, and rabbits for food for his family.

Philip was well aware of the battles to the east and to the south, for the most part from trips to Pearson's for supplies or from the very rare trips he made to Bemis Tavern for a pint. If anyone were to ask, he would acknowledge that the colonies were at war with Britain principally over the issue of self-rule. However, it was not until a stop at the tavern on the way out of the woods by mid-August that he heard the news that there was a formal declaration of war to which all of the colonies unanimously agreed called the Declaration of Independence.

━━◦◦◦◦◦━━

After the battles of Concord and Bunker Hill, and before June of 1776, as many as twenty battles had been fought between the British and the Patriots from Quebec through New York and New England, to South Carolina, Virginia, and Georgia, with each side winning as many as they lost.

On a hot and humid 7th day of June, 1776 in Philadelphia, the three-part resolution called The Resolution for Independence composed by the Fifth Virginia Convection was presented to the Second Continental Congress by Virginia delegate Richard Henry Lee and formalized a position to be adopted by the colonies proclaiming that the Thirteen Colonies in America were free and independent states. Further, the resolution called upon the congress to form foreign alliances and prepare a plan for a colonial confederation.

Custodian Andrew McNair opened the tall windows to let in a breeze. The breeze was warm, but the movement of the air gave some relief, even though it also brought in the flies and mosquitos to add to the delegate's discomfort. Despite the discomfort of the Philadelphia summer weather, the resolution was met with vigorous debate. Although it was unlikely that a resolution would be reached with Britain, opponents argued such a declaration was premature and the congress should direct their attention to securing foreign support for the cause first. Supporters of the resolution argued the opposite, saying that such a petition for foreign aid to the government of an established country would most certainly be viewed as asking that country to get involved in an internal British struggle. This, they said, made it more imperative that they declare independence first. Many members also felt the colonies were already at war with Britain, or some even saying that they were already independent and that such a declaration was merely a formality and unnecessary.

Many felt that the power and protection of Britain was necessary for the survival of the fledgling colonies. Some feared what they felt would most assuredly be an imminent invasion from France, referencing the separation of the colonies from British protection as an opportunity for France to seek retribution from their defeat in the French and Indian War. Further, some suggested that such a separation might even result in civil war.

With many of the delegates being evangelical Christians, some even with seminary degrees, there were arguments on religious grounds. Members of the Church of England viewed the revolution as not only an act against England, but as an act against The Church and God as well. Further, the Quakers, whose religious beliefs were against violence of any kind, much less a full military engagement, objected vehemently, their strong presence in the Pennsylvania delegation forcing a negative Pennsylvania position.

The debate got so heated that some colonies threatened to not participate and to leave should such a declaration be accepted. Finally, after much discussion and debate, John Hancock, the president of the congress, declared the discussion closed. The matter was temporarily settled by tabling the motion for three weeks. This also provided the delegates time to report on the proceedings of the convention and the positions on independence of the various delegates back to their colonial governments and to consolidate the support of their individual colony legislatures.

It was also agreed that a committee be formed to prepare a draft document defining and explaining colonial independence. This Committee of Five, as it was called, consisted of John Adams of Massachusetts, Benjamin Franklin of Pennsylvania, Thomas Jefferson of Virginia, Robert Livingston of New York, and Roger Sherman of Connecticut. A general outline was agreed to by the committee and it was suggested by Adams that the committee name Jefferson, the member most qualified to compose such a document, be the documents primary author.

The first draft was entitled, A Declaration by the Representatives of the United States of America, in General Congress Assembled. Adams would contribute much but told Jefferson why he should be the one to write it.

"Reason first, you are a Virginian, and a Virginian ought to appear at the head of this business. Reason second, I am obnoxious, suspected, and unpopular. You are very much, otherwise. Reason third, you can write ten times better than I."

———◁◁◁◁◁∫▷▷▷▷▷———

At the end of June, the congress was reconvened with the first business being the resumption of the discussion and debate regarding The Resolution for Independence.

The arguments from a month ago resurfaced. As a thunderstorm forced all the windows to be closed, the air in the room became even more stifling than usual. The old arguments re-emerged! John Dickinson of Pennsylvania rose and made a lengthy speech declaring such action as independence premature. He argued again such a declaration brought the threat of invasion by France or the possibility of civil war. John Adams as the leader of the cause for independence was relentless in calling every dissenter to task. His keen insight into each delegate's personal views, as well as the economic, religious, and social culture of each colony, enabled him to tailor the tenor of his argument individually to each colony and delegate. Despite his often-caustic speech, he proved to be highly effective as well as highly respected. Finally, whether it was the stifling heat and humidity in the room, or that President Hancock felt all the arguments had been presented and fully discussed, Hancock called for a preliminary roll call vote to determine the status of the views of the colonies regarding the issue of independence.

Although the number of votes granted each colony varied based on its size, it was agreed by the Congress that the vote for independence must be unanimous with each colony having one vote. The vote by each colony was to be decided by majority vote of the delegates within the colony. When the vote of the seven person Pennsylvania delegation was taken, three other delegates supported Dickinson in voting no, with Benjamin Franklin and two other delegates voting yes for independence. Pennsylvania was joined in voting no by South Carolina and Delaware with New York abstaining. Delaware was forced to vote no because their delegation of three had been reduced to two by the absence of Caesar Rodney who was suffering with cancer, with the remaining two delegates split. New York, the most predominantly Loyalist colony had the most to lose by a possible defeat in a war for independence. Further, even if the motion was not carried, a vote for yes would surely result in occupation of New York by Britain, and the delegates themselves would most certainly be considered guilty of treason and put to death. Thus, when the vote of the congress was tabulated, nine colonies voted in favor of independence, three dissented, and one, New York, abstained.

The president then called a mid-day meal recess asking the delegates to reassemble in two hours to take up further debate before a final vote on the motion. Many of the delegates gathered at the City Tavern where they were accustomed to caucusing between and among themselves. Word from General George Washington, appointed by the Congress as Commander in Chief of the Continental Army just about a year earlier, arrived reporting that on June 14th, the order had been given for the American forces to retreat from Canada to Fort Ticonderoga on Lake Champlain. In addition, he reported, and it was passed on by the patrons at the tavern, that over a hundred British warships had arrived in the New York harbor. The largest invasion force of which anyone had ever heard had thus arrived in order to squelch the rebels who were threatening war in order to gain independence from the crown.

With the occurrence of this event, when the delegates reconvened, a sense of urgency seemed to pervade the congress, and the dynamics of the congress began to change. Pennsylvania's John Dickinson seemed to have recognized that patience and pleading with the king was now no longer an option and decided to vacate his attendance from the congress. Robert Morris decided to join Dickinson and to not further attend the congress also. The absence of these two men aligned Pennsylvania with the rebels. The youngest delegate at twenty-six years of age, Edward Rutledge of South Carolina, had been caucusing with his delegation, hoping to convince the other delegates to vote in favor of the declaration. The arguments on each side became briefer and more repetitive, as one might expect. Sensing this new feeling of urgency among the delegates, in the hope that he had convinced his fellow South Carolinian delegates to vote yes, on this second day of July, Rutledge called for a final vote. The motion was accepted, seconded, and approved.

President John Hancock ordered Secretary Charles Thomson to call the roll. Suddenly the doors burst open, and Caesar Rodney rushed into the room, his boots spattered, and his coat drenched from the rain. When he had become aware of the split in his delegation, he mounted his horse and rode the eighty miles to Philadelphia through thunder, lightning, and rain, determined to break the tie vote within his delegation. Exhausted, pale, and hungry, with the pain of cancer pounding in his jaw, he made his way to his delegation and dropped into his chair.

When the room quieted once again, the secretary continued the roll call. New Hampshire voted yes followed by Georgia. When Delaware was called next, Thomas Mc Kean helped Caesar to his feet. Both men voted yes, negating the no vote of George Read. With the absence of Dickinson and Morris, the Pennsylvania vote became a yes. Only South Carolina and New York stood in the way of a unanimous yes vote. Surprisingly, South Carolina changed its vote to yes. Apparently, the young Rutledge had been successful in convincing the South Carolina delegation to change their vote.

Once again, New York abstained. The logic of New York's vote seemed questionable at best since their single no vote would have prevented a fight for independence, and surely the British would be aware of such. Thomson handed the results to Hancock. With the single abstention, the vote was again declared unanimous. When the results were read, the Assembly Room broke into cheers. The president of the Second Continental Congress prepared a statement, rose, and hammered the session back into order.

Resolved that these united colonies are, and of right ought to be free and independent states. That they are absolved from all allegiance to the British Crown, and that all political connection between them and the state of Great Britain, is, and ought to be, totally dissolved.

The room erupted into cheers as the delegates congratulated each other.

⊸⊸⊸⋙⋘⊸⊸⊸

With the issue of independence resolved, it was now time to review, edit and revise Jefferson's draft of the Declaration of Independence to the satisfaction of all thirteen colonies, a formidable, if not a seemingly impossible task indeed. The editing process was agonizingly slow with each suggested revision debated ad nauseam. The preamble, unchanged, began:

We hold these truths to be self-evident; that all men are created equal; that they are endowed by their Creator with certain inalienable rights; that these are life, liberty and the pursuit of happiness; that to secure these rights, governments are instituted among men, deriving their just powers from the consent of the governed.

The document was edited and modified principally by Adams and Franklin, but also by many others over the next two days into the morning of July 4th. After two days of several agonizingly time-consuming revisions, many of a trivial nature, each breaking the heart of Jefferson, it appeared that the time for approving the final draft had arrived.

However, the issue of slavery, the elephant in the room that had been avoided by all, could be avoided no longer. Jefferson's version of the declaration called for the abolition of slavery. The issue was finally brought to the floor by the delegates from Georgia and South Carolina, the only two colonies still active in importing slaves from Africa. Although most slaves were owned by plantation owners in the southern colonies, one third of the delegates were slave owners themselves, including some delegates from the north where abolition was more widely approved. Most northern states favored gradual emancipation laws to slowly phase out such practice. Jefferson's document had called slavery a cruel war against human nature itself. Discussion went on for several hours with discussion ultimately turning into argument. The argument seemed to have reached its peak with a final plea from John Adams who had never owned a single slave.

"How can we, on the one hand agree that all men are created equal and are endowed by our creator with certain unalienable rights including the right to life, liberty and the pursuit of happiness, and on the other hand, with one voice, justify denying more than a hundred thousand Africans of such rights."

"Oh, how self-righteous we are," came the cry from an unidentified delegate from the back of the room, unrecognized by the chair, although one would guess that the cry came from the Georgia or South Carolina delegation. "You self-righteous slick tongued wolves in sheep's clothing from the north line your pockets with gold derived from transporting these so-called equal Negroes from the African continent to the American continent."

The room burst into loud raucous conversations, outbursts and shouting of support or objection to what the delegates had just heard.

"Order, order!" commanded the congress president, John Hancock. As the noise in the chamber slowly diminished and finally subsided, Hancock continued.

"Apparently, the heat and humidity of the day has taken control our informative and respectful demeanors and replaced them with our tempers. Although a brief thirty-minute recess will not allow us the opportunity to lower our external temperatures, hopefully it will allow each of us to lower our internal temperatures and will thus effect a return of civility to these proceedings." Still mumbling and grumbling, the delegates exited the chamber.

It was apparent that this assemblage of thirteen slave owning colonies were deeply divided on the issue. Both colonies from the north and the south had a profound commercial interest in preserving the trafficking and trading of human beings. The southern plantations needed free labor to produce tobacco, cotton, and other cash crops for export to fuel its economic engine. The northern shipping merchants were dependent on trade with Europe and Africa, including the trafficking of African slaves.

During the recess, John Adams lingered behind, slumping into his chair with his head in his hands. Benjamin Franklin, whom Adams respected, but was not necessarily a close friend, approached Adams from behind and put his right hand on Adam's left shoulder. "John, may I have a word?" The fiery leader of the movement for independence slowly raised his head, turning to face Franklin, wiping his brow.

"Yes, Dr. Franklin, what is it?"

"John, we must put this issue behind us. We must not take our eye off the target. We must not be denied our goal over such a controversial issue. Our goal is independence. I am sure there is discussion now among some colonies regarding withdrawing their support. We must save this battle over the abolition of slavery for another day."

Franklin dropped his hand from Adam's shoulder, turned, took a few steps away, putting his hand under his chin, turned again, and returned, placing his hand on the shoulder of Adams once again.

"You have heard the story of the old bull and the young bull, have you not, John?"

"No, I do not believe I have, but most assuredly I am about to," he replied with a relaxed smile.

"Well, now it seems there was a young bull and an old bull standing together atop a hill. The hill overlooked a ravine which was occupied by several cows. The young bull turned to the old bull and said, 'Let us run down the hill and enjoy the favor of one of those cows.' John, do you understand what I mean by enjoy the favor?"

"Yes, my kind sir, I am fully aware of the difference in your intended meaning of such a phrase in the animal world versus its conventional meaning in the world of humanity. Continue with your story, please."

"Very well, then the old bull turned to the young bull and said, 'No, let us walk down and enjoy the favor of them all.' John, take it from this old bull. It is time to walk down this hill. These are proud men, all of some achievement. Slavery or not, we must live with them and the citizens of these united colonies they represent."

"So be it," Adams replied as he rose with a smile. Placing his left hand on Adams right shoulder, Franklin reached out his right hand to Adams. The men interlocked right hands without any further words being uttered.

As the recess ended, the delegates slowly shuffled back into the room in the oppressive summer heat and humidity, some singularly, some in conversation in groups of two or three, many wiping the perspiration from their foreheads and the back of their necks. When the delegates were seated, the convention was reconvened with Chairmen Hancock hammering his gavel and declaring the congress in session.

"Gentlemen, this body will now come to order. The issue at hand is the...humpgh... (clearing his throat) DISCUSSION.... on the paragraph in the declaration regarding the abolition of slavery. We shall resume discussion in a respectful and informative manner."

Dr. Benjamin Franklin rose to his feet.

"Mr. Chairman, may I make a motion?"

"The Chair recognizes the delegate from Pennsylvania."

"Mr. Chairman, I move that we eliminate the paragraph from the document relating to the abolition of slavery which begins with the words, He (King George III) has waged cruel war against human nature itself, and ending with the words, paying off former crimes committed against the liberties of one people, with the crimes which he urges them to commit against the lives of another from the declaration."

"Is there a second?"

"I second the motion," replied John Adams as he rose to his feet. There was a brief hum of several low conversations among the delegates followed by a deadly silence.

"Is there any discussion on the motion?" A pause of several seconds followed as Hancock's eyes surveyed the room......still, deadly silence.

Hancock continues. "Absent any discussion, all in favor signify with the raise of a hand, one hand from each delegation.

A delegate from each of 12 colonies raises his hand.

Hancock surveys the room again and makes a written note. "Any Opposed?" ..... once again, deadly silence. After a few seconds the only sound heard is a chair sliding backward over the floor. A delegate from New York rises.

"New York abstains."

"The chair declares that the motion has passed unanimously. The paragraph cited will be eliminated from the document." The gavel came down hard.

Once again, the room erupted into cheers as the delegates congratulated each other. Now all fifty-six members of the Second Continental Congress, in the eyes of Britain, had committed treason against the crown and their lives, the lives of their families, and their properties were all at risk of dire consequences.

After about a month's recess, the Declaration of Independence adopted by the thirteen colonies on July 4th, was signed by the delegates on August 2nd. John Hancock, as President of the Continental congress, was the first to sign. After signing in large bold letters, Hancock declared, "His majesty can now read my signature. He will not need his glasses. Gentlemen, we must now all hang together."

Benjamin Franklin added, "Yes, we must indeed all hang together, or most assuredly, we shall hang separately."

Cheers and congratulations between and among the delegates followed. Some of the delegates fell to their knees, placing a bible on top of the document. Many wept. Several prayed, followed by a moment of silence. Fifty-two of the fifty-six signers were Evangelical Christians. About half had seminary degrees. Five had sons who were pastors. Samuel Adams, cousin of John Adams, said, " We have this day restored the Sovereign to Whom alone men ought to be obedient. He reigns in Heaven from the rising to the setting sun, may His kingdom come."

After the declaration was signed, it did not take long for the word to reach Saratoga, and it was the topic of discussion at Pearson's on a day shortly thereafter when Philip heard the news on a routine trip to the store to get supplies. As he left the store, Philip decided that he needed to talk to Drew Gerard. He knew he would understand his dilemma. He was the only person with whom he could discuss such personal matters as he had done his whole life as if he were his blood brother. When he arrived at Drew's blacksmith and iron working shop, Philip saw several horses tied up at the barn hitching rail so he knew that Drew must be inside. As he approached, the barn door was partially open, and he noticed the profile of a woman in an embrace with Drew. Not wanting to surprise or embarrass Drew, Philip quickly back tracked to the house and called out to Drew.

"Drew, are you there? It is Philip."

"Yes, come on back."

Philip walked back to the barn, and Drew and Sally Bemis appeared in the doorway of the barn. Philip suspected that Sally was the woman in Drew's arms, remembering that on his first visit to the tavern some 10 years ago, Drew had left the table to visit with Sally in the back room, and that she had also asked for Drew on his last visit to the tavern with his friends soon thereafter.

Drew and Sally were holding hands, and Sally greeted Philip with a big smile and a rather coy tilt of her head.

"Hello, Philip, nice to see you again after all these years."

"Hello, Sally, it is good to see you. Hopefully, I am much wiser now than then, but I am not sure that much wisdom can be gained in the wild where I have spent most of time since that day, we spoke in your father's tavern so many years ago."

Drew never spoke of Sally back then, and Philip was certainly not aware, nor could have anticipated how much Drew and Sally's relationship would grow while his life was spent in the wilderness as a long-hunter.

"I'm sure we are all much wiser now," she replied as she gazed up into Drew's smiling face and he slipped his arm around her waist.

Thinking to himself, Philip now realized that obviously this was one more reason why Drew wanted to move his black smith shop away from his farm. For whatever reason, he wanted to keep his relationship with Sally close to the vest.

"Well, now you know all there is to know about us, but what brings you by?" Drew replied, obviously not wanting to talk about Sally and him any longer. "You have a look of concern."

He greeted his little brother with a hug, which Philip energetically returned, both men swaying left to right and back again.

"Sit....sit," Drew ordered, pointing to a bench a few feet away. "How is Renee? I hear she is with child. Too bad your mother and father are not here to enjoy and spoil their new grandbaby. I am sure they will silently enjoy their son's first child, their first grandchild, from where they are in the house of the Lord."

Philip lowered himself to sit on the bench and looked back and forth from Drew to Sally and back to Drew once again. "I truly believe that also, so that troubles me not."

"So then, from that comment, I surmise that something is troubling you, and it is the reason for your visit. So, please share it with me."

Seeing that Philip was hesitant to talk about what must have been a very personal matter, Sally excused herself.

"I'll be in the cabin," she said over her shoulder as she left the two close friends alone. Hanging his head and resting his head in his hands with his elbows on his knees, once Sally was out of earshot, Philip declared, "It is this situation between the colonies and Britain."

Smiling at first at Philip's use of the word, situation, and then, with the smile slowly turning into a frown, Drew replied, "I'm afraid it is more than a situation. The Continental Congress has declared independence. It is expected that the colonies will be invaded both by land from Canada and by sea. Is that what is troubling you?"

"Why must men always seek power over others? When will there be an end to war? I am content, and I am wealthy in my contentment, for as Locke says that he is richest who is content with the least, for contentment is the wealth of nature. And Socrates said that men are by their nature, free. I do not wish to take sides. I wish to be left alone with my life and my freedom."

"I agree with all that you and our friends, Locke and Socrates, profess, but they each said much more. Socrates said that only the dead will know the end of war, and I am afraid he is as correct today as when he said it. And sadly, I believe it will be true so long as there is life upon this earth."

Rising as he spoke, and putting his hand on Philip's shoulder, Drew added, "Let me remind you, Locke tells us that if the legislature abuses power, it forfeits its power to the people, and revolution becomes society's obligation. I agree that men are by their nature free, but to protect that individual freedom, sometimes we must take sides. Once again, as Locke said, not to choose sides favors the aggressor."

As Philip rose, he queried, "Drew, what do you think I should do?"

Drew walked toward his anvil, and picking up his hammer replied, "Well, perhaps you can remain neutral until the violence threatens you, your family, and your property. If and when that occurs, and I believe it will, you will have to decide whether to side with your fellow colonists, as I, and join them in their fight against the aggressor or join the aggressor. Unfortunately, only you can make that decision."

"I must think. You have not made it any easier, but I guess no one can." Philip strode toward his horse and climbed into the saddle. He pulled the reins to the left, and waving, gently nudged the horse down the path to the river road.

As he did so, Drew shouted, "I have simply reminded you of what your books taught me. Think long and hard. I know that, with God's grace, you will make the right decision." He returned the wave and went back to his work.

CHAPTER 7

In the fall when the last harvest was complete, Renee was becoming physically uncomfortable and anxious to bring her first child into the world. Then, one rainy night in mid-October, Renee awakened and rolled over to awaken Philip.

"It's time, Philip."

"When? Right now?" Philip asked only half awake.

"No, we have a while, but it will be soon. I think you should get Martha and bring her here. It's not that I don't think we can handle it without her, but it is comforting to have another woman...."

Before she could finish her sentence, Philip was out of bed and pulling on his trousers.

"You shall get no argument from me, my love. I will be back before you realize I am gone."

With that brief response, Philip laid a rifle by Renee's side and was out the door followed by Soldat, who would stand guard as usual until Philip's return.

"Stay, Soldat. Take care of Renee," he commanded as he pointed to the bed where she was lying. Soldat returned to Renee's bedside and lay on the floor beside her as Philip closed the door behind him.

In less than a minute Philip went to the barn and was astride his horse. He did not want to take the time to hitch the horse to the wagon. As quickly as one could travel the few miles to the Pearson store in the darkness and rain, Philip found himself behind the store, banging on the door of the Pearson's living quarters. There was no immediate answer, so Philip resumed banging on the door. Finally, although it seemed like hours to Philip, within moments Mr. Pearson was at the door. Without opening the door, Pearson shouted, "Who goes there? What in God's name brings anyone to my door at this hour?"

"It's Philip Eames, Mr. Pearson. Renee is in labor. Can Martha........"

Before he could finish the question, the door opened, and Sam Pearson, with one hand on the door and holding a lantern in the other, shouted over his shoulder to Martha,

"Martha, it's Renee, she's ready to deliver. Come quickly," turning to Philip, he added, "Come in Philip. Martha will be here in a few moments."

"If you don't mind, sir, I'll just wait here."

"As you wish, lad." Pearson replied, turning and climbing the stairs to the living quarters, but leaving the door open.

As Pearson walked away, the light from the lantern faded, and within a few moments Philip was standing in darkness with only the light of the moon outlining objects near at hand and the sound of crickets filling the otherwise silent night. Soon the lantern came back into view, becoming brighter and brighter as it came closer and closer. This time, however, it was carried by Martha. As Martha exited and closed the door, she descended the steps, and doused the lantern, leaving it on the stoop. Philip spoke first.

"Martha, I'm sorry to...."

"Shush, Philip. Let us be on our way."

Philip climbed up into the saddle and then helped Martha up behind him. As they cantered around the store and to the river road, the rain subsided. As the clouds drifted off to the north, the moon helped light the way. Martha could not help but think back to that day, when, as children, she and Philip rode to school in the same manner as she and Philip were now riding. It was just about the time when Philip had run the boys off who were bullying her that she became too grown to sit in front. The only thing that could have caused Martha to be happier than she was right at this moment was to be giving birth herself to her and Philip's child, rather than helping to deliver the child of Philip and another woman, albeit a woman to whom she had grown so close.

As soon as Philip was out the door, Renee placed the kettle on the fire in the fireplace to boil water so it would be ready when he returned with Martha. Then she climbed back into bed, placing the rifle next to her side. She began counting in French between the contractions to gage their frequency, as well as to pass the time. When a new contraction would begin, she would grimace and shout the last number to no one into the darkened room, lit only by the fire under the bubbling kettle. The old hound dog knew something different and unsettling was occurring and paced back and forth from the bed to the fire, looking up at Renee and whining after each grimacing cry. Just as the pain of the last contraction became almost unbearable, she heard the thumping of horse's hooves outside, coming closer and closer. Perspiring heavily, she raised herself up, leaning on one elbow, and lifted the rifle to a near firing position.

The door opened, and, laying the rifle down and sitting up, she gasped, "Martha... Ahhhh....... Philip."

"Renee," Martha replied, "Lie back and try to relax," as she removed her shawl and rushed to Renee's side.

"Relax? I cannot relax."

Philip lingered by the door, sheepishly and asked, "What do you want me to do?"

"Just take Soldat and go outside and stand guard," Martha replied. "We will call you when we need you."

Willingly, Philip did just that, sitting on the steps outside the little house, one hand on his musket, the other on the hound reclining at his side. For over thirty minutes, he could hear the agonizing and painful cries of his beloved wife, feeling that he was responsible for her suffering. Each time he heard Renee cry out, Soldat would alternately look up into Philip's eyes and whimper as if to ask, "What should I do," and then lay his head on Philip's leg. Suddenly, Philip could hardly hear a sound coming from inside, the chirping of the crickets now being louder than the sounds coming from the house. Then, after seemingly an eternity, but in reality only about ten minutes, when he was sure he could not bear the frustration any longer, the door opened and Martha appeared, smiling. Philip let out a sigh of relief.

"You can come in now, Philip, and meet your son."

Philip raised himself quickly, paused a moment next to Martha, squeezing her hand in an unconscious gesture of appreciation. Soldat reached Renee's bedside before Philip. As she turned her head toward the animal, Soldat licked her face several times and then laid down on the floor by her head. Somehow, she felt her father had sent her a kiss through his faithful soldier. Philip paused, watched, and then moved quickly to Renee's side. He gazed down at mother and child as Renee looked up and reached out her hand. "Philip," with his and Renee's eyes transfixed, brought her hand to his chest as he lowered himself to kneel by Renee's side. As if planned, in unison they both transferred their eyes to their newborn son, and, after a moment of wonder, Philip bowed his head and the new parents kissed tenderly.

Martha watched momentarily, voyeuristically sharing the moment, but then becoming embarrassed, though unnoticed when she realized something very personal for Philip and Renee was occurring. She turned her gaze away and busied herself with cleaning up, burying an emotion she could not explain beneath her breast.

After several moments, when she heard both Philip's and Renee's voices and low laughter, Martha approached the couple, wiping her hands on a towel.

"Philip, I'm sorry to interrupt you at such a time, but I need to ask you to take me home now. The sun will be up soon, and I have to open the store."

Renee looked up and extended an arm to Martha. Her other arm still cradled the baby. Philip turned, looking at Martha over his shoulder and reached out his hand to her.

"Martha, come!" Renee commanded.

Martha walked toward Philip and Renee, reaching out to grasp both extended hands. She lowered herself smiling, and all three embraced.

"Martha, you will always be a part of our family. I do not know what we would do without you. I love you. Thank you," Renee whispered with tears in her eyes.

"And I love you," Martha replied as she lowered her head and kissed Renee.

"For some time, 'til now, she has been my only family," Philip advised.

Philip and Martha rose. Philip bent at the waist to kiss Renee one more time. "I will return quickly. Rest until I return. Keep the rifle close by and listen for Soldat."

Philip and Martha exited the little house followed by the old hound who reclined himself in his usual spot just outside the door. Philip mounted his horse and then reached down to hoist Martha up behind him. As they rode back up the river road to the store, Martha leaned forward, somewhat exhausted, but with a feeling of euphoria as she wrapped her arms around Philip's waist. Philip was anxious to return, but feeling Martha leaning against his back, he knew that he should try to keep the ride as smooth as possible. When they reached the store, they could already see a light inside, as Martha's father readied the store for the daily opening. Martha slid down from behind Philip. Philip reached down and clasped Martha's extended hand. She wrapped both hands around his. They exchanged goodbyes, and Martha ascended the steps to the store, turning to wave as she opened the door, and then quickly disappearing from sight as the door closed behind her. Philip turned and slowly cantered the horse away from the store, but as soon as the store was out of sight, the canter turned into a full gallop as Philip raced back to his wife and newborn son.

Renee, half asleep, heard someone mounting the steps and knew it was Philip since there was no warning from Soldat, only a whimper as he sought a pat from his master and slipped through the door beside him. As Philip entered the house and approached her bedside, Renee smiled and finally closed her eyes and fell asleep, exhausted from the ordeal she had just experienced. Philip adjusted the covers around his wife and the child she cradled by her side. He arose and stared down at his wife and child through the flickering light from the fireplace for several moments in quiet admiration.

The harsh northeastern winter soon returned with all its fury. Once again, Philip and Renee were often snowbound for days or weeks. Philip was able to make some hunting trips to replenish the supply of fresh meat when the weather permitted and chopped firewood to keep the little house warm. Staying close to the fire, this time the young couple was totally preoccupied with nurturing their child. Renee was surprised but pleased with how attentive her rugged frontier woodsman husband was to their child.

Although the war with the British continued to grow in intensity, the battles were some distance away, and it was only on his infrequent trips to Pearson's store when he could get through the snow that any thoughts of the events of the struggle which were discussed around the stove entered his mind.

It was on one such trip that Philip learned of Continental Army General Washington's activities in New Jersey. Most of the group around the stove were Loyalists who had previously forced the few who were sympathetic to the Rebels into silence as they boasted of Washington's retreat from Fort Lee in New Jersey to the Delaware River in November. On this day, however, they had to listen to the emboldened loud voices of the previously silent minority when Washington's troops were victorious in the Battles of Trenton and Princeton during the early months of the New Year before both sides went into hibernation throughout the winter. At this point, the discussions, although somewhat loud at times, were still political in nature without anger or malice on either side. By the time he was out the door and on his way home, all such thoughts usually evaporated quickly.

It was not until a trip to the store in May that Philip would hear of anything related to conflicts between Britain and the colonists that he could not shake off. Washington had remained hunkered down in Morristown, New Jersey well into the month of May. However, it was on a trip to the Pearson store to acquire seed for the spring planting that Philip learned that, although the British had launched a successful raid on the colonists' supply store in Danbury, Connecticut, a small group of militia men were able to drive the British back through Ridgefield to the Long Island Sound. Philip realized that each time he heard anew of the ongoing conflicts, they were moving closer and closer to Saratoga, and for the first time he started to have concern that the war against Britain might well threaten his family and their way of life. This time what he had heard on his routine supply trip lingered.

"My dearest Philip, I understand well your desire to not commit to either side in this disagreement between the colonists and the crown, but I fear that, as the fray comes closer and closer to our little world that we will have to soon take sides," Renee implored as Philip tried to explain his indecisiveness on his return from the Pearsons.

"Renee, you most certainly are correct, but I am pulled in opposite directions by so many forces that I remain tortured both day and night, and it unfortunately renders me paralyzed. I truly understand the inequities and unfairness that my fellow American citizens speak of relative to our treatment by the motherland, and on the other hand, the tradition of my family and my father's service to the king pulls me in that direction. I am more an American than an Englishman and have a profound love for what this land offers me. I am a woodsman, a long-hunter, and now a husband, a father, and a farmer as well. I have no interest in what the style of life in England might have to offer. If it were not for my love for you and Robert, I would surely retreat to the forest until this conflict were over. It is there that I truly feel closer to God than even in Reverend Framingham's church. I believe God put us here and gave us free will to choose between right and wrong, good and bad. We each have the opportunity to enrich our lives in a manner which reflects our own individuality and the responsibility to enrich the lives of those we love and of other humankind around us. My mother taught me that there is something of God in all of us, and that each human being has a special worth different than that of any other human being. She taught me to seek truth in my inner experience with God and that my conscience should be the basis of my morality. Because of this, I take the commandment, 'Thou shalt not kill' literally. God has commanded me to never kill another human being!" he declared as he paced the floor, imploring her understanding.

"Philip, each day I realize that you are truly much more than what you claim to be, a simple woodsman and farmer. Truly, the books that General Schuyler gave you as a youth and your mother's teachings have had a profound effect on you."

"My dear, you may well have identified the true source of my dilemma. I always felt that the ideas and ideals of those much smarter than I, conveyed to me in those writings, and as a child through my mother's teachings, had enriched my life and made me a better man. But now I feel that, perhaps if I had never been exposed to such influences, my life would be much simpler and my decision much easier."

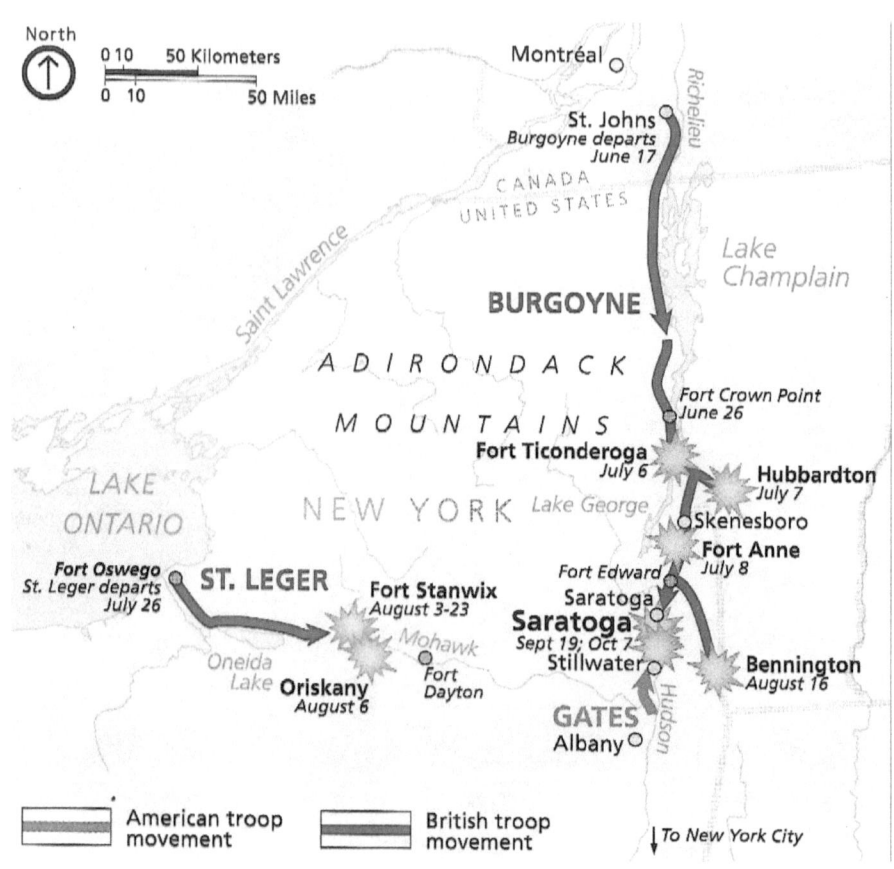

North

0 10   50 Kilometers

0   10   50 Miles

Montréal

St. Johns
*Burgoyne departs
June 17*

Richelieu

CANADA
UNITED STATES

Saint Lawrence

BURGOYNE

*Lake
Champlain*

A D I R O N D A C K

M O U N T A I N S

*Fort Crown Point
June 26*

Fort Ticonderoga
July 6

Hubbardton
July 7

LAKE

ONTARIO

N E W   Y O R K   *Lake George*

Skenesboro

Fort Anne
July 8

Fort Oswego
*St. Leger departs
July 26*

ST. LEGER

Fort Stanwix
August 3-23

Mohawk

Fort Edward   *July 8*

Saratoga

Saratoga
Sept 19; Oct 7

Bennington
August 16

*Oneida
Lake*   **Oriskany**
August 6

*Fort
Dayton*

Stillwater

Hudson

GATES
Albany

American troop
movement

British troop
movement

↓ *To New York City*

Saratoga National Historical Park Visitor's Guide

CHAPTER 8

John Burgoyne's ship, the Apollo, docked in the Quebec harbor on May 6, 1777, marking the third time he had arrived on the North American continent. The water shimmered and glistened from the reflected sunlight as his ship slipped into the harbor surrounded by tall imposing pine and maple trees with picturesque mountains in the distance. Regiments, clothed in their British uniforms assembled to greet him and framed the Apollo's arrival. As the ship approached the dock, it was an impressive sight. Equally impressive was the tall handsome Lieutenant General John Burgoyne, in his scarlet red coat with gold piping, a white waistcoat, and shiny black boots. Gentleman Johnny, had arrived at the continent for the third time. He brought with him reinforcements and all the tools of war. As he descended the gangplank, he acknowledged the cheering regiments lined up to greet him.

—⚊⚊⚊—

John Burgoyne entered the British Army at 15 years of age as a junior officer. In his early twenties, after serving with distinction in the Seven Years War in Spain, in 1761 he was elected to Parliament in the House of Commons and again in 1768. During this period, he had earned a reputation as a man about town, a womanizer, a gambler, and a drinker, as well as a lover of the theater. In fact, he achieved modest a success on the British stage as a playwright with his play, *Maid of the*

Oaks. However, his theatrical fame never reached the level of success of his military career. In London he met Lady Charlotte, the youngest daughter of the Earl of Derby. They were forced to elope because of her father's opposition to their marriage. At 28, unable to pay his gambling debts and the living expenses on a captain's pay, he sold his commission and sailed to France with his wife. French aristocrats enjoyed entertaining the daughter of an English Earl and her handsome debonair husband. By 1756 the couple reconciled with Lady Charlotte's father, and they returned home to England where Burgoyne was able to purchase a captaincy in the 11th Dragoons. Because of his fair treatment of his men, Burgoyne earned the nickname, Gentleman Johnny, and rose through the ranks from captain to colonel in a less than four years. By 1772, Burgoyne was promoted to major general and three years later, on April 19, 1775, when Britain's General Gage ordered seven hundred British soldiers to Concord, New Hampshire to destroy the colonists' weapons depot, Burgoyne was dispatched to America for the first time on May 25, 1775, with fellow Major Generals Howe and Clinton with Burgoyne as second-in-command under General Clinton. There he observed the Battle of Bunker Hill. Frustrated by the loss of so many men at the battle, as well as earlier at the battle at Lexington and Concord, along with Clinton's refusal to delegate him any authority, he decided to return to England. Before leaving, however, he was able to gain an audience with Lord Rochford, Secretary of State for the Colonies.

"And to what do I owe this pleasure, General?" greeted the secretary.

"If it be your pleasure, my lord, I would want to discuss the state of affairs with the few but bothersome rebels here in the colonies."

"Yes, yes, it's truly troublesome and very annoying. What do you have in mind?"

"Well, my lord, these rebels are truly in the minority, and that the vast number of the colonists are loyal to the king. Further, for the most part, the unrest seems to be concentrated here in New England. I truly believe that we should dispatch a large army of such foreign troops as might be hired to begin their operations on the Hudson River with another army composed partly of old undisciplined troops and partly of Canadians, to act from Canada, a large levy of Indians, and a supply of arms for the blacks, to awe the southern provinces conjointly with detachments of regulars."

"And what do you feel might be accomplished with such an ambitious plan?"

"Well, my Lord, such a force, supported by a numerous fleet to sweep the coast, might possibly do the business in one campaign."

"I must say this sounds quite interesting and quite plausible, and I shall convey your thoughts to the king. I am sure he will seek advice from his military advisors and the Secretary of War and give it serious consideration."

In November of 1775 John Burgoyne returned to England. With no word regarding his plan, Burgoyne was ordered to return to North America for the second time in the spring of 1776 as secondincommand to General Guy Carleton, Governor of Canada, where he was once again frustrated by his lack of authority. During June of that year, Burgoyne was devastated by the death of his wife of twenty-five years in England. Carleton had managed to defeat General Benedict Arnold's rebels at the battle of Valcour and drive them from Crown Point, their staging point for their navy on Lake Champlain. Arnold was forced to abandon the post and fall back to Fort Ticonderoga. Having taken control of the lake, Carleton quickly occupied Crown Point. However, after lingering for two weeks, he determined that it was too late in the season to continue the campaign and withdrew north into winter quarters. Though a tactical defeat, the Battle of Valcour Island in October of 1776 was critical strategic victory for Arnold as it prevented further invasion by the British from the north.

Disgusted with Carleton's decision and lacking any real authority, Burgoyne requested and received permission from Carleton to return to England just after the Battle of Valcour Island to settle pressing personal matters. While there, he visited his wife's grave who was buried next to their only child, who had died at the age of ten. He was also able to settle many family and financial matters.

Once back in England, he also repeated the plan in his document, 'Reflections upon the War in America.'

In this document, he offered, "I have always thought Hudson River the most proper part of the whole continent for opening vigorous operations. Because the course of the river, so beneficial for conveying all the bulky necessities of an army, is precisely the route that an army ought to take for the great purpose of cutting the communications between Southern and Northern provinces, giving confidence to the Indians, and securing a junction with Canadian forces. These purposes effected, and a fleet upon the coast, it is to be morally certain that the forces of New England must be reduced so early in the campaign to give you battle upon your own terms or perish before the end of it for want of supplies."

The plan was for a force to move south along the Lake ChamplainHudson River route to Albany. There they would be met by a force led by General William Howe moving north from New York City with a sizable army of his own. Colonel Barry St. Leger would provide support by leading a smaller force east from Lake Ontario through the upper Mohawk Valley to Albany. Joining forces there, New England would be cut off from the rest of the colonies, thus halting the rebellion where it began before it could gain any further traction.

On December 10th, Burgoyne met with Lord George Germain, perhaps the king's most influential minister, and, presenting him with this document, was able to convince him of the inevitable success of his plan to quell the rebellion on the American continent. His plan was finally approved by the king and his ministers, placing General Burgoyne in charge of the troops to move south from Canada to Albany.

———

Over the next two weeks after his arrival on the American continent in 1777, Burgoyne and his entourage made their way to Montreal where he was met by Governor Guy Carleton. Having previously served under the governor and relegated to only minor duties, Burgoyne took personal but unspoken pleasure in delivering the letter formalizing his command of the British force in its invasion of the colonies from the north. The governor concealed his outrage and treated the General Burgoyne with civility, but at the same time reminding Gentleman Johnny that as long as he was governor, he outranked him.

The governor kept his hard feelings to himself and held a ball in honor of the new commander in the Chateau Ramezay, the ostentatious residence of former governor, Claude Ramezay, which coincidentally was the same venue where a similar affair was held by General Benedict Arnold, welcoming Benjamin Franklin and the Catholic commissioners sent to Canada in an attempt to convince the Canadians to join the colonies in the struggle against the British.

Shortly thereafter, Burgoyne's regiments moved south to St. John's and presented Carleton, still not thrilled with his replacement by Burgoyne, with a full military review. The following day Burgoyne reviewed the details of the plan of the mission ahead with his top officers, Brigadier General Simon Fraser, Brigadier General Henry Watson Powell, Major General William Philips, Brigadier General James Hamilton, and Lieutenant General Friedrich von Riedesel. Eager to get started, they all responded enthusiastically.

Early on morning of June 24th, drums sounded the order to march. Two cannons were fired from the deck of the Maria to signal the beginning of the northern attack on the colonies. If one were not aware that this was the commencement of a major military engagement, one would have concluded that he was observing a full military review and parade. Leading this backwater armada out of Cumberland Bay up Lake Champlain were four hundred native warriors in birch bark canoes with full war paint and colorful feathers framing their heads. Following them in formation came various contingents: the Advanced Corps under Brigadier General Simon Fraser composed of regulars in scarlet coats and white breeches and waistcoats; gunboats with artillerymen dressed in blue; light infantrymen in black leather coats and red waistcoats; grenadiers with bearskin headgear; the British brigade in scarlet coats faced in yellow, red, or white.

Next came the tall, masted ships, the Royal George and the Inflexible followed by two schooners, five other vessels, and a fleet of twenty-four gunboats. Rowing behind them came the First Brigade under Brigadier General Henry Watson Powell made up of the 9th, 47th, and 53rd regiments. Three small light sailing vessels came next, each with a general, Burgoyne in the central craft, flanked on the left side by Major General William Phillips commanding the British Advanced Corps, 1st and 2nd Brigades and Lieutenant General Friedrich von Riedesel on the right, made up of the German Advance Corps, 1st, and 2nd Brigades.

Rowing next was the British 2nd Brigade, made up of the 20th, 21 and 62nd regiments under the command of Brigadier General James Hamilton. Bringing up the rear came the German mercenary dragoons also under General Friedrich Adolf von Riedesel with their officers in plumed caps, grenadiers with tall miter caps faced with shiny metal plates, infantrymen in dark blue coats, white breeches and waistcoats, followed by jagers (riflemen) in green uniforms with red cuffs and facings.

This full contingent of about 9,000 men was made up of about 4,200 British regulars, 4,000 German troops, and approximately 1,000 loyalists, Indians, Canadians, and camp followers composed of soldiers' wives and children, as well as laundresses and sutlers (men who earned a living by selling provisions to the soldiers). This was an impressive military force indeed. Generals von Riedesel and Simon Fraser would be leaned upon very heavily by Burgoyne, both reporting directly to him. Von Riedesel, a rather short stout man with rosy cheeks, rose to his rank quickly after capturing the attention of Frederick the Great, King of Prussia, in battles on the European continent. Brigadier General Simon Fraser, born in Scotland was a handsome man in his late forties when he arrived in America to serve with General Burgoyne. A successful leader and tactician in the British army known for his bravery, he became a quick friend of Burgoyne.

That evening, Burgoyne penned a proclamation to be circulated throughout New England. In it he promised protection to the Loyalists, while at the same time he threatened those who resisted their advance with the vengeance of the Indian forces available to him. The proclamation only served to anger the colonists and brought him ridicule when word got back to England. He did however forbid his native allies from attacking old men, women and children, and prisoners, pretty much to no avail.

American held Fort Ticonderoga would be the first, if not the most difficult test of the British plan. The fort, located at a narrow near the south end of Lake Champlain originally built by the French was captured by the British in the French and Indian War in 1759. However, it was now commanded by the Rebels after being captured by Benedict Arnold and the Green Mountain boys in a surprise attack two years earlier.

What he could not have known, however is that in the autumn of 1776, General Philip Schuyler had written a letter to the Continental Congress detailing the northern department's urgent needs. The list included basics such as provisions and money to pay the troops, and maintenance items such as wooden boards, planks, and pitch and oakum for ship repairs. He also requested 6,000 additional troops, 2,500 for assignment to Fort Ticonderoga.

Colonel Anthony Wayne, known as Mad Anthony for his fearlessness in battle, in command at Fort Ticonderoga, reported to General Schuyler that during the ensuing winter he had hardly enough healthy men to post pickets. He was losing troops daily from something that came to be known as camp distemper with symptoms including chills, fever, aching joints, nausea, dysentery, and loss of appetite. Daily, men froze to death in their tents or outside their tents from exposure to the elements.

General Schuyler sent petitions to congress repeatedly for assistance to remedy these dreadful conditions, all falling on deaf ears. In the spring of 1777, on June 18th, Schuyler came up to the fort from Albany to examine conditions for himself. What he found left him in shock and dismay. He found the garrison of men miserably clad and armed, and reported many of them were literally barefooted and most of them ragged, and without blankets as well. Many lacked bayonets, substituting sharp pointed poles and sticks. Many of the huts were burned for firewood during the winter.

With the troops down to a mere 2,500, when all agreed 10,000 were needed to defend the fort and nearby Mount Independence, a council of war including General St. Clair, replacing Wayne, who was extremely happy to be replaced under the circumstances, agreed it was prudent to prepare for a retreat to Mount Independence. Also, at about the same time, it was finally decided that an effort should be made to fortify the area around the fort. With the efforts of every man available, it was estimated that the task, which included completing a footbridge and boom to obstruct the enemy's approach from the lake, in the opinion of military engineer, Tadeusz Kosciuszko, would take at least six weeks.

It was the intent of the Continental Congress, ever since the capture of the fort, that the British invasion from the north be stopped right here. With British ships on the lake reported by scouts to be forty-two miles north of the fort, the question remained, as the old saw goes, "Will the guests arrive too late to the party?"

Soldat rose from his resting place at the foot of the large maple tree near the southeast corner of the house. His ears perked and a low groaning sound came from his throat as he became aware of a horse and rider coming up the path from the river road to the little farm. Hearing Soldat's groan, Philip looked up from the ground he was tilling south of the farmhouse to see the horse and his rider jogging up the path to his little farm. He followed Soldat to the top of the path to meet his visitor who was now close enough to be recognized as his childhood friend, Michael Emerson. Michael dismounted his horse, dropped the reins, and as the two men briefly embraced, Soldat sat at their feet looking up at both men. Philip was recalling his conversation with Michael in Pearson's store several months ago. As they stood face to face, Michael placed his right hand on Philip's left shoulder.

"Philip, the British are invading from Canada. They have over 7,000 troops and several hundred Indians. It is their plan to sail down Lake Champlain toward Albany and cut off New England from the rest of the colonies. They believe that if New England can be isolated, they can be subdued, and this rebellion may well be over before it goes any further. I am going north to join them, Philip. Come join me."

Philip dropped his head. As he lifted his head to face Michael, Michael dropped his hand from Philip's shoulder as Philip's left arm swept towards his little farm home, palm up.

"Michael, I am a farmer, not a soldier. I have a family now. Before that, I was a hunter and a trapper. I hunted, and yes, I killed animals for their hides and meat. I have never killed a man. Surely our leaders will find a way to settle this thing without further bloodshed so that we can all get back to our lives."

"Philip, leaders on both sides have been talking for years. It has not worked, and I am convinced it will not work. This is the quickest way to resolve it. I understand your position, but this is something I have to do."

"What does your father say?"

"I haven't spoken to him about it. I left him a note. The time has come when I must be a man and make my own decisions. You had to become a man because you had no choice. Both of your parents are gone. I must become a man through choice, and this is my choice."

Michael turned and mounted his horse. As he led the animal toward the river road, over his shoulder he shouted, "You will see, Philip, this will all be over soon. Wish me God speed."

Philip waved to his friend, but Michael was too far away to hear a response. Philip replied in words hardly above a whisper.

"God speed, my friend, and I pray God keeps you safe." He dropped his head towards the ground and returned to his work. Soldat returned to his resting spot under the maple tree.

———

Brigadier General Simon Fraser's troops led the advance to Crown Point expecting to meet the first encounter of the invasion with the colonists. Instead, they found an abandoned fort. They set up camp and waited for the remaining forces to catch up to them. Michael Emerson had no way of knowing at what point in his northern trek that he would meet up with the British forces, so his plan was to keep driving north going up the west side of Fort Ticonderoga through identifiable trails and on towards Crown Point about ten miles north of the fort until he encountered them. He hoped he would be able to identify their location from a distance perhaps by campfire smoke so he could determine the best way to approach the British encampment. However, he never got the opportunity. Within a few miles of Crown Point, before he saw any signs of the British camp as he rode into a clearing, a British infantryman stepped into his path from the protection of the forest.

"Who goes there? Throw your firearm to the ground and raise your hands above your head."

"Michael Emerson, a loyal subject of the king. I wish to join your forces."

Michael dropped his musket to the ground and raised his hands in the air as directed. The British sentry picked up Michael's musket and circled around behind him.

"Okay, dismount and follow the trail to your left until you see the tents."

Michael did as he was instructed, leading his horse behind him. After about a quarter of a mile, they entered the encampment, and passed a row of several tents.

"Okay, halt! Drop the reins." Once again, Michael did as he was instructed.

"March forward to the next tent."

As they approached the adjacent tent which was set back a few feet from the rest, Sargent Reynolds, a tall refined looking man in his mid-thirties was guarding the tent. He entered the tent and returned with General Fraser.

"What do you have here, soldier?" inquired Fraser.

"Says his name is Emerson, Sir. Says he wants to join us," replied the sentry.

"Forgive my men, Mr. Emerson. I am General Fraser. What is your given name?"

"Michael, sir. Michael Emerson, loyal subject of the king."

"Where are you from? Are you familiar with this area?"

"Saratoga, sir. I have been up this way a couple of times with my father as a youth. I remember a hill that provides a very commanding view of the fort and surrounding area, and I believe I can find it again."

"And what does your father do?"

"He's a farmer in Saratoga, sir."

"Give back this man his firearm, Private. Emerson, we're going to give you a chance to serve the king and to get to know Private Smiley here," Fraser replied, pointing to the sentry. "Private, take young Emerson and scout up ahead toward Fort Ticonderoga. See if you can find Mr. Emerson's hill and see what you can find out about the geography, the terrain, and the Rebel forces there. Sergeant Reynolds, find someone to replace Private Smiley at his post."

"Yes, sir," replied Smiley. This way, Emerson. We'll get some supplies first and then be on our way."

"Yes sir, at once, sir," replied Reynolds, as he saluted, turned, and left in search of a replacement for Smiley. General Fraser turned and reentered his tent.

Michael led Smiley the ten miles or so through the mosquitoes, black flies, underbrush, and occasional marshlands to Mount Defiance, the hill of which he spoke, about a mile southwest of the fort. This hill provided a strategic command of the fort and excellent view of the Rebel positions. There was only one problem in getting troops to this position. The hill required an almost perpendicular ascent to reach the top. Michael and the sergeant took mental note of the fort and its surrounding geography.

Retracing the difficult route back to Crown Point, they returned to report to General Fraser. Smiley confirmed Michael's observations, but also reported the almost impossible ascent to the top, not only for troops, but for heavy artillery as well. Fraser immediately asked his adjutant to fetch Lieutenant William Twiss, an engineering officer. Smiley and Emerson again described what it would take for them to make it to the peak.

"Sir, it's quite a feat for even a goat, more so for a man," concluded Smiley.

"Well, Lieutenant, what do you think?" queried the general.

"Where a goat can go, a man can go; and where a man can go, he can drag a gun," replied Twiss.

Within hours Fraser's forces pulled out, advancing about three miles north of Fort Ticonderoga and setting up camp at the place where Burgoyne had landed his forces on July 1st on the west side of the fort.

The usually gregarious and outgoing Burgoyne would normally take pleasure in inviting at least a guest officer or two to his tent for dinner. This was not the case this night. Fatigued by the last few day's travels, he elected to take his dinner alone in his tent. He was eager to remove his British officer's coat, laden with medals which made it even heavier and uncomfortable after a long day. He loosened his shirt and lay down on his cot. Abigail Simpson, traveling with the British army, an attractive shapely auburn-haired woman in her thirties and the wife of Captain William Simpson, volunteered to serve the general his dinner. As she entered the tent with a flask of wine in one hand and a wine glass in the other, Burgoyne rose from his cot to a sitting position.

With a coquettish glance and a teasing smile, she offered,

"Good evening, General." While not necessarily the first thing a gentleman of your stature would prefer to relax him after a hard day and a long journey in a strange land, perhaps a glass of wine would rank a close second.

She threw her head back, and at the same time as the general laughed, she giggled like a young adolescent girl. She exited and entered the tent several times to retrieve utensils and serve different courses, bending over in front of the general to reveal her bosomy charms as they laughed and spoke somewhat suggestively and tauntingly to each other. At the conclusion of the meal, as she was exiting the tent with dishes and utensils, General Burgoyne asked if she would like to return and share a glass of wine with him. Throwing her head back once again, she agreed with a flirtatious smile. After returning with more wine and a second glass, the guard outside the tent heard giggling and laughter and then noticed the light inside the tent grew dark without the waitress leaving.

Before dawn the next morning, Abigail Simpson slipped away unnoticed except for a nodding glance from the guard.

The following day, Burgoyne put his planned attack on the fort into motion. The German left wing went ashore on the east side of Lake Champlain. He ordered Fraser to take his Advanced Corps to take Mount Hope, northwest of the fort, blocking a possible escape route to Lake George. Riedesel was to circle around Mount Independence and block the road to Hubbardton to engage any Rebel reinforcements from New Hampshire. Soon after noon, St. Clair and his troops abandoned Mt. Hope, falling back to the log fortifications of the old French lines from the French and Indian War. From the east side, the Germans had to cross a mosquito infested marsh and managed to advance less than a mile the first day, but there was no good escape route in that direction. Rebel forces blasted the British troops from the fort as they were landing supplies and preparing for their siege against them.

CHAPTER 9

On the third day, following the assessment by Lieutenant Twiss, General Fraser ordered British soldiers to clear a path up the nearly perpendicular side of Mount Defiance. On July 4th, taking a full 24-hour day, British soldiers were able to clear a road up the side of Mount Defiance, and the army's oxen dragged a pair of cannons, 12-pounders, to the top of the hill. Fraser's advance was unnoticed until a fire built by some of the Indians revealed the British position at the peak of the mount.

This signaled General Arthur St. Clair, a former British officer, now the American commander of the fort, not only of the near proximity of the British, but that the guns atop Mount Defiance could open fire at any time. He also was almost certain that Mount Independence would be attacked at the same time. After holding council with his officers, St. Clair decided to abandon the fort. That night, heavy guns from the fort opened fire on the British to divert their attention while the fort's troops loaded two hundred boats with supplies, baggage, wounded troops, and camp followers.

At 3am, with the New Hampshire Regiment manning the boats, the besieged defenders of Fort Ticonderoga departed quietly away from the fort. Disobeying orders, one of St. Clair's officers set his headquarters on Mount Independence on fire, turning the retreating soldiers, thinking their retreat would be discovered, into an angry mob. The British and German soldiers saw the fire atop the mount and notified General Fraser.

Fraser's Advanced Corps set out in pursuit across the partially burned bridge crossing the waterway between Mount Independence and the fort, but they were slowed by the narrow road south with potholes, ruts, and stumps, not to mention the heat and mosquitos.

By about 1:00 pm, St. Clair's fatigued army stumbled into Hubbardton, twenty miles southeast of Mount Independence. While his troops rested, St. Clair waited for his rear guard to arrive. After two hours, deciding it was not going to happen, he pulled out leaving a portion of his men to wait for rear guard and the 2nd New Hampshire Regiment. When they arrived, they were to follow the main army to Castle Town, stopping just outside the village for the night. Three hours later they arrived with a thousand men in worse shape than St. Clair's main force. Instead of following St. Clair, they decided to stay in Hubbardton for the night.

Miles behind the retreating rebels, Fraser stopped his advance to give his troops a rest. While encamped beside a stream, and after finding and butchering two bulls to feed his troops who had not eaten all day, Riedesel arrived at camp with his jagers. He announced that his corps bringing up the rear would arrive soon. The generals decided that Fraser would push on for another few miles while Riedesel's men would rest where they were for the night. At 3:00 am the next morning, Fraser moved out and Riedesel followed in support, bringing up the rear.

Early on July 7th, Fraser had almost caught up to St. Clair. When his scouts reported the Rebels were just over the hill,

Fraser decided to act immediately instead of waiting for Riedesel. While the unaware Rebels enjoyed their breakfast along a brook, someone suddenly shouted, "The enemy are upon us!" From part of St. Clair's forces behind a stone wall, and some forming a position on the right flank, the rebels forced back a British charge. With the British left flank threatened, Fraser realized he was in a most precarious position, outnumbered and with the Americans holding the high ground. A detachment of British grenadiers was able to claw its way up Zion Hill. Holding a commanding position, the Rebel forces were forced to fall back behind a log fence. Nonetheless, the fighting intensified, and Fraser knew he was in serious trouble. However, Riedesel with his jagers and grenadiers arrived in time to save the day, driving the Rebels scurrying into the woods. The 45-minute battle inflicted about two hundred casualties on the British and about 390 on the Americans.

Meanwhile, the escaping American flotilla leisurely made its way to Skenesborough believing the boom across the narrow pass between Fort Ticonderoga and Mount Independence would slow the British long enough for them to reach Skenesborough without fear of being attacked. British gunboats had smashed the boom, chain, and bridge easily and the British force was in hot pursuit. Catching the rebels totally off guard, Burgoyne's gunboats attacked the Rebels destroying three Rebel boats while two craft surrendered. Supplies and provisions hauled from Ticonderoga destroyed or captured, the Rebels retreated further south heading to Fort Anne with about 190 men from the British 9th Regiment in pursuit. On July 7th, the British attacked, and a fierce two-hour battle followed with the British running low on ammunition. However, the Rebels, thinking British reinforcements had arrived, set fire to the fort and retreated 16 miles further south to Fort Edward.

Burgoyne felt his campaign had reached a pivotal moment. He now had a decision to make. He could return north back to Fort Ticonderoga and, by taking a water route to Lake George and crossing over land for a short distance, ultimately continue on south by resuming a water route via the Hudson River. However, he did not relish the idea of retreating north to Fort Ticonderoga before advancing south once again, so he announced to his troops, "This army must not retreat." He remained in Skenesborough for the next two weeks.

About a week before he renewed his advance southward, five hundred western Indians arrived. A recurring problem the British had with their Indian allies was the practice of scalping. The taking of a scalp as a trophy enhanced an Indian's status as a warrior. They also felt that by taking of a scalp of their victim, they were placating the spirit of the dead. Not only the British, but the civilized world considered such a practice to be barbaric and disrespectful of human dignity. At a welcoming feast, once again Burgoyne addressed the natives to remind them that, although it was acceptable to scalp enemy soldiers killed in battle, prisoners, women, children, and old men must be spared from this practice. The speech was interpreted by his Indian agent and spoken to the Indians in their native tongue. To discourage scalping, he promised them a bonus for every live prisoner they brought into camp. Also once again, however, the order fell on deaf ears.

On July 24th, Burgoyne left Skenesborough with his troops heading south for Fort Anne. Rebels slowed British progress by clogging the road to Fort Anne and Fort Edward by felling trees, destroying bridges, creating man made swamps by digging ditches to drain water from bogs into their path, and by blocking Wood Creek with boulders. The British forces reached Fort Anne two days later.

At Fort Anne, two warriors arrived with a blonde scalp. Blonde hair was not very common in the area, and a Loyalist officer, David Jones, suspected it belonged to his fiancée, Jane McCrea. It was not clear what had really transpired, but what was clear was that Miss McCrea's fiancé, was devastated. Burgoyne's Indian agent explained that two Indians vying for the bonus he had announced for capturing prisoners like Miss McCrea alive got into an argument regarding who had earned the bonus, and somehow in the fray, Jane McCrea was shot. One of the Indians then took her scalp. Burgoyne was livid!

Screaming at De Luc, his French Indian agent, he shouted, "These Indians are savages! I will have no more of this."

That night he sent a note to General Gates: "The news I have just received of the savages having scalped a young lady, their prisoner, fills me with horror. I would rather put my commission in the fire than serve a day if I could suppose government would blame me for discountenancing by some strong acts such unheard of barbarities."

Calling General Fraser and De Luc into his quarters he demanded, "This murderer must be executed!"

"Sir, I would not be so hasty," replied de Luc.

"I beg you to reconsider your decision. Consider instead the consequences of such a decision."

"What in God's name do you mean? I cannot tolerate such barbarian behavior any longer!"

"Such an act would certainly cause mass defections among the Indians. They will most certainly defect and either go over to the Rebels or head home and attack white settlers as they do so."

Fraser agreed saying, "Sir, instead, I suggest all future raids by the Indians be led by an officer."

Burgoyne accepted the suggestion and ordered that such a procedure be carried out. Considering past behavior and the fact that the British officers and the Indians did not communicate very well, to say the least, this certainly seemed an improbable solution.

The British resumed their trek south arriving at Fort Edward two days later to find the fort abandoned. The Rebels had left the fort and retreated farther south. Once again, Burgoyne reminded his Indians about killing innocent people.

Although they nodded their heads in agreement, the next day the western Indians headed home. News of the incident by word of mouth and by stories published in local newspapers created increased defections from the British cause among the Loyalists and increased numbers of volunteers to the American cause.

To make matters worse, Burgoyne was further bogged down by the fact that the further he moved south, the longer his supply line from Canada was stretched, a situation which would only get worse.

Already short of supplies and hearing about a large stockpile of supplies available in Bennington, Vermont from a Rebel defector, he sent a young scout on horseback ahead to Bennington to determine what was available and the size of the protective force. The young scout was able to attain the information he sought, mainly through idle conversation at a local Bennington tavern and was excited to return to Fort Edward with the news. Because of his excitement, on his return he forced his steed into an unwise and unnecessary gallop along a narrow path atop a cliff. The horse stumbled, turning its ankle on a rock. The young scout was thrown over the cliff and knocked unconscious. In doing so, the young man suffered a broken leg as well as serious internal injuries. A rider heading west on the same path saw the scout's horse nibbling on some grass in a clearing above the cliff. He dismounted his horse to try to discover why the saddled animal was alone in the clearing. Cautiously looking about, he wandered over to the cliff and discovered the young man lying on his back at the foot of the cliff.

Finding a steep path down the side of the cliff, by holding on to branches and shrubs he was able to make it to the scout's side. He lifted the young man's head and determined that he was breathing. He spoke to him softly, trying to revive him into consciousness. Then, as the young man responded, the well-intentioned rescuer brought his canteen to the lips of the wounded scout. Bleeding heavily from his side, choking on water and blood, he tried to speak. The rescuer cradled the young man's head in his arms and lowered his ear within inches of wounded man's mouth.

The young man whispered his message, meant only for British General Burgoyne's ears at Fort Edward, into the ear of his well-intentioned rescuer. Choking on his own fluids, coughing and gasping for air, he breathed his last breath. His head went limp in the arms of his anonymous rescuer.

The scout could have had no idea to whom he had passed this information of which side, if any, the recipient was a part. If nothing else, he knew only that his well-intentioned rescuer was a Good Samaritan. Without anything with which to dig a grave, this Good Samaritan covered the young scout's body with rocks, placed at his head a cross hastily made from a small dead tree branch and knelt and said a prayer. He mounted his horse, and with the dead scout's horse in tow, headed for Fort Edward.

Late in the afternoon, he slowed the horses as the fort came into view about a quarter of mile in the distance. Stopped by a pair of sentries as he approached the fort, the rider offered his weapons without being asked and requested an audience with General Burgoyne.

"I have some valuable information for the general that he is expecting," he offered.

"What's your name, and what is the message?" asked one of the sentries.

"The general doesn't know me, and the message is only for his ears."

"Then why should I bring you to him if he does not know you?"

"He is waiting for this message. If I were the enemy, would I just walk up to you and offer you my weapons?"

"Hold him here," the sentry demanded of the other sentry. "I will see if the general wishes to see him or if we should just serve him to the wolves," he added with a smirk.

The sentry who was to hold the messenger laughed, grabbed the messenger by the sleeve and led him to a bench.

"Sit!" he ordered with a little shove.

As he sat, the messenger's foot hit something that had the sound of metal. He looked down to determine the source of the noise and spotted a button from a British soldier's uniform. With the sentry looking away, for no reason at all other than to acquire a souvenir, he bent over, picked up the button and placed it in his pocket.

The other sentry returned.

"Okay, the general will see you."

The accidental messenger followed the sentry to Burgoyne's headquarters.

"I understand you have a message for me?"

"Yes sir," the messenger replied.

Then he told the story of how he had come upon the general's scout and the information he had relayed to him.

"So, tell me, young man, how did you come upon my scout? Who are you, where are you going, from where, and for what purpose?"

"My name is Peter Framingham. I am a silversmith apprentice from Bennington returning to Saratoga to care for my father who is ill."

The general, without a reply, slowly walked to the door, opened it, and addressed the guard outside the door.

"Bring General Fraser to me, please."

Within a few moments General Fraser entered the room.

"General," Burgoyne started, addressing Fraser.

"Yes, sir."

"We had a young Loyalist scout from Saratoga that aided us at Ticonderoga, did we not?"

"Yes, sir, we did."

"Is he still with us?"

"Yes, he most certainly is."

"Bring him to me. He may be able to help us again, but in a different way."

Without question, General Fraser left the room momentarily and returned with Michael Emerson.

"Peter," Michael blurted out with a grin as he rushed to Peter Framingham and embraced him.

"So, you know this Framingham fellow, I see?" asked General Burgoyne. "And how do you know him? Can you vouch for him? Is he with us?"

"Why, yes sir. Peter and I are both from Saratoga. We grew up together. We've spoken of our loyalties often, right Peter?"

Peter nodded. As always, Peter's nod was all Michael required.

"Very well. Now, Peter, what is the message you have for me?"

"As you might expect sir, your scout was able to say very little with the condition in which I found him, but his dying words were that I should convey to you that the supplies you need are bountiful in Bennington and guarded by only 400 men."

"Thank you, Mr. Framingham, your information shall be most helpful to his majesty's forces."

With a hand on the shoulder of both Michael and Peter, Burgoyne ushered them to the door.

Once outside, walking together towards Peter's horse, Michael asked, "Peter, where are you headed? I thought you were in New England somewhere."

"I was," Peter, always a man of few words, replied. "My father is ill, and I am going to Saratoga to help my mother care for him."

"Oh, Peter, I am so sorry. Please tell Pastor Framingham that I am praying for him and give your mother my best."

"Thank you, Michael. I will." The men embraced. Peter mounted his horse, waved, and rode away leaving the dead scout's horse behind.

On August 4th, Burgoyne ordered a contingent to embark on a mission to capture the huge stockpile of American supplies at Bennington guarded by only four hundred men, as reported by Peter Framingham. At their disposal, the British army had 374 Brunswick infantrymen, three hundred Indians, thirty Hessians, several Loyalists, and two 3-pound cannons.

Peter Framingham, however, did not head for Saratoga but steered his horse back in the direction from whence he came, to Bennington! Once arriving in Bennington, he had little trouble in identifying the commander of the forces assigned to defend any attack on Bennington and its stockpile of supplies as General John Stark. Peter took a day to attend to a personal matter that he felt should be addressed before he approached the general. The next day he walked into General John Stark's Bennington headquarters.

⸺◦≺◦◦⸺

Originally a farmer, General Stark had been a successful British officer during the French and Indian War as a lieutenant with a Special Forces military unit called the King's Rangers, more commonly known in the colonies as Roger's Rangers. He left the Rangers in 1760, retiring as a captain and settling in Derryfield, New Hampshire. Following the Battle of Bunker Hill, he returned to active duty as a colonel commanding the 1st New Hampshire Regiment in March of 1775, serving along with Major General William Prescott during the Battle of Bunker Hill and in the battles of Trenton and Princeton later in March of 1776. General George Washington himself was impressed with Stark, and Stark replaced General Enoch Poor when Poor refused to have his regiment join the Battle of Bunker Hill. Despite his refusal to serve at Bunker Hill, Poor was promoted over Stark.

Feeling he had been passed over by Poor, who had less combat experience and had no will to fight, Stark resigned his position in disgust, returned to his farm, and married Molly Page. In the summer of 1777, John Stark accepted a commission as Brigadier General of the New Hampshire Militia only on the condition that he would not be answerable to the Continental Army. He immediately reported to Manchester, New Hampshire, where he assembled a force of around 1,500 men.

———

Once again, Peter found himself requesting permission to see a general directly involved in the war for the colonies' independence. Insisting that he had a message that had to be delivered to General Stark in person, he was detained as permission was sought.

"The general will see you. This way," directed Peter's escort as he led him down a narrow passage to the general's quarters.

As he entered the room, the general, looking out of window with his back to Peter, turned to face him with his hands behind his back.

"I understand you have a message for me," General Stark stated in a rather matter-of-fact manner. "And you are?"

"Peter Framingham, a silversmith apprentice from here in Bennington, Sir."

Then Peter told the story of his recent trip and how he had come upon the mortally injured British scout and his meeting with Burgoyne, probably stringing together more complete sentences that he had ever uttered in his life at any one time.

"However, sir, I told General Burgoyne that there were 400 men guarding the supplies here, when, in truth, his scout told me that there were roughly eighteen hundred," Peter concluded.

"And why should I believe such a tale?"

Peter was silent for a moment, and then he reached into his pocket and withdrew the British officer's uniform button he had retrieved back at Fort Edward. He handed it to the general.

"Well, this does show that you were either in the presence of a British soldier or at least at a place where he lost his button," Stark replied with a smile after examining the button closely and handing it back to Peter.

Peter then reached into his other pocket and withdrew a piece of paper which he handed over to the General. The General read the document confirming Peter's enlistment in the New Hampshire Militia written and signed by his enlisting officer the day before.

"Thank you," replied Stark. "I believe you will fit in just fine. I see that you are a man of few words. Well, that's okay. A war was never won with words. As it is said, actions speak louder than words, and your actions have already spoken loudly and have contributed to our effort."

With his hand on Peter's shoulder, General John Stark led his new recruit to the door, knowing he must ready his troops for an attack.

On August 9th, Burgoyne dispatched a contingent of 1,200 men to Bennington made up of Germans, Loyalists, and Indians under German Lt. Col. Friedrich Baum. The force captured a grist mill nine miles outside of Bennington. From prisoners, Baum heard that there were 1,500 men defending the supplies, not four hundred as earlier reported. Not knowing who to believe, nonetheless, Baum sent a letter to Burgoyne to tell him about the suspected increased number of American soldiers at Bennington and about the capture of the mill.

Heavy rains the next day forced Baum to dig in and wait for reinforcements. Stark had already received additional reinforcements and prepared to encircle the British forces and attack from all sides. He sent a group of men to take out the British guarding the bridge over the Walloomsac River from the south. When the remainder of the American troops heard gunshot from the bridge position, this was the signal to attack.

Stark cried, "We'll beat them before the night is out or Molly Stark will be a widow."

The bloody fight that ensued lasted about two hours. In addition to Baum's ammunition running low, the ammunition wagon caught fire and exploded. Many of the troops had been killed or wounded or had deserted. Baum was mortally wounded, and his remaining troops forced to surrender.

As Stark's troops were scattered around the battlefield plundering the enemy, the British reinforcements appeared. The Rebels were in no shape to take on this new challenge, but fortunately reinforcements arrived from Manchester just in time. After heavy exchange of fire, the mercenary German forces, running short of ammunition, were routed. At the end of the day, the British had suffered over nine hundred casualties while Stark had suffered about seventy.

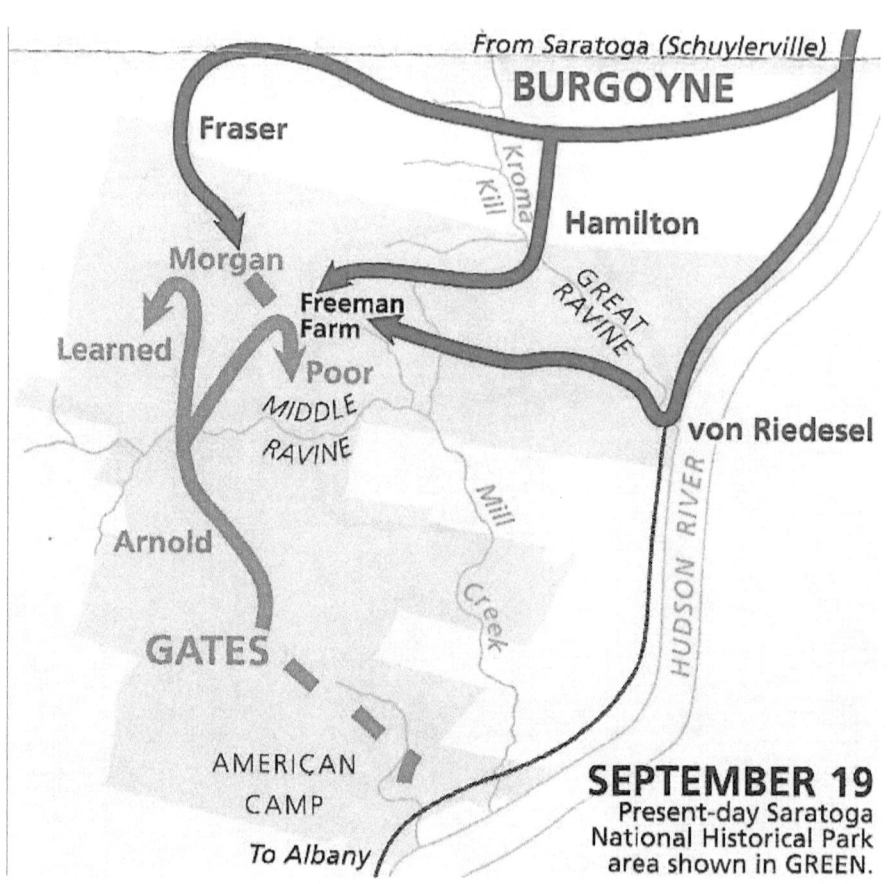

Saratoga National Historical Park Visitor's Guide

CHAPTER 10

On July 23, 1777, contrary to the plan to head north to rendezvous with General Burgoyne in Albany, British Gen. Howe, with 15,000 men, set sail from New York for Chesapeake Bay to capture Philadelphia. He left only a small force in New York under General Clinton to proceed north to aid Burgoyne. This move was sure to drastically affect the course of the war.

Britain's Colonial Secretary, George Germain, approved the movement to Philadelphia in the belief that Howe would return to New York in time to cooperate with Burgoyne. Howe was already at sea and deeply committed to the Philadelphia campaign when he got Germain's endorsement, thus making the troops best positioned to help Burgoyne unavailable in the numbers needed by his plan for a successful conclusion. Without a supporting force with the numbers required, Burgoyne's army could become isolated in the hostile North American wilderness.

If this change of plans was not enough, St. Leger had halted his advance down the valley to besiege Ft. Stanwix. In the battle of Oriskany on August 6th he stopped an American column marching to aid the fort. However, when he heard that a strong force under Benedict Arnold was on its way to confront him, St. Leger halted the siege and retreated north toward Canada. Finally, if the defeat at Bennington was not a fait accompli for Burgoyne's plan, it certainly came close. He was now faced with a serious decision!

Should he cut off all contact with Canada and press forward with his advance toward Albany or should he retreat to Canada with his mission a failure.

On August 19th, ex-British officer, now American Major General Horatio Gates, arrived in the American camp north of Albany at the convergence of the Hudson and Mohawk Rivers to take over command from Major General Philip Schuyler. Schuyler had been removed from command because of the poor state of Fort Ticonderoga as well as the troops stationed there and the loss of the fort to the British a few weeks earlier. Schuyler was blamed for the although he had reported the poor conditions there several times to the Continental Congress and was denied funds and troops to remedy the situation at what was once an Americans stronghold.

General Gates found that he had inherited a 4,500-man army plagued with sickness and resulting low morale. However, the numbers grew daily. A combined force of twelve hundred men under General Benedict Arnold and a corps of riflemen under Colonel Daniel Morgan were dispatched by George Washington to aid Gates. Gates named Arnold second in command with Morgan reporting directly to Arnold. In addition, militia companies began pouring into camp swelling the number of men to 7,500.

Gates and his army moved north first to Stillwater and then on to Bemis Heights at the southern edge of Saratoga, a more defendable position. There, atop the wooded plateau, the American army had command of the single road to Albany, a narrow passage squeezed between the hills and the river and offered visibility in every direction as far as the eye could see. American artillery on the heights and in redoubts along the Hudson flanked the shores of the river and commanded the road, fortifying the site.

In events to the south, on September ninth through the eleventh of 1777, in the Battle of Brandywine Creek, General Washington and the main American Army of 10,500 men were driven back toward Philadelphia by General Howe's British troops. Both sides suffered heavy losses, and Congress was forced to vacate Philadelphia and resettle in Lancaster, Pennsylvania.

Burgoyne made his decision. On September 13th, despite the setbacks, Burgoyne decided to push forward to Albany. He crossed to the west bank of the Hudson at Saratoga and began marching southward. Although the east side would have offered less Rebel resistance, the river would have to be crossed at Albany where it was much wider and deeper, giving an advantage to the American troops in wait. Also, the dismantling of the bridge behind the German troops after they had crossed the river, for all intents and purposes, had cut off all communication with Canada.

Once arriving on the west side of the river, the Burgoyne's first task was to locate a suitable sized clearing to serve as a camp. An advance scouting party had located the ideal location on the land of the Sword farm just north of Saratoga and reported back to General Burgoyne. It turned out to be more than ideal when it was determined that Mary Sword, now in charge of operating the farm with her husband away in prison, was herself a Loyalist and offered to supply the troops with whatever they needed that her farm could provide.

Mary's husband Thomas originally arrived on the North American continent to serve with the British in the French and Indian War as a lieutenant. Deciding to remain after the war, he purchased the fifty-acre farm and operated it for several years. When General Schuyler petitioned him to serve in the Continental Army as an officer, and he refused due to his Loyalist leanings, he was arrested and imprisoned in Albany.

As the British troops marched down the river road to their newly acquired camp, they passed Drew Gerard's cabin. Once they were off the river road and busy setting up camp, Drew made his way down the river road to notify the Pearsons along with Philip and Renee of the arrival of their new neighbors. The Pearsons readied their cellar as a bunker to be used if needed and Philip assured Drew that he was going nowhere and would be standing on guard to protect his family for the foreseeable future. With that, Drew returned to his cabin to prevent the invading troops from confiscating his property.

In the early morning hours of September 19, 1777, as soon as the sun had burned off the heavy fog, British General John Burgoyne launched a threecolumn attack against General Horatio Gates and his American forces. The bellowing of cannons announced the advance of the British troops to the Rebels on Bemis Heights. While two divisions headed through the heavy forests, the third, the German troops, took the left flank marching down the river road. American scouts detected the British movement and notified General Benedict Arnold and General Gates.

General Gates, having served as a British officer, had a characteristic disdain for the sloppy appearance of the Continental Army officers. He admired, instead, the crisp bright red uniforms of the Brits and their sharp lines in battle rather than colonial marksmanship from an Indian style ambush from the protection of a forest. Gates longed to replace Washington as Commander-in-Chief of the army and had lobbied Congress for such a promotion just as he had lobbied to replace Schuyler. Arnold could care less about any of that. His desire at this point was simply to win!

—⟨⟨⟨⟨⟨⟩⟩⟩⟩—

At thirty-six, a stocky five-foot nine handsome man with piercing gray eyes and coal-black hair, Benedict Arnold was considered by many, including General George Washington, a military genius. He was also known for his temper, and a propensity for drunkenness and rage. All agreed, however, one was unlikely to find his equal on the field of battle, and no American commander had more success against the British than he. He was even worthy of admiration in his only defeat attempting to capture the English fortress at Quebec in 1775, leading his troops through the uncharted wilderness of Maine in the dead of winter. There, he had earned the nickname, The American Hannibal. Well into the second year of war, the Continental Army was transforming from an untrained militia into a professional fighting force. Perhaps this was the single reason that this undisciplined former merchant and smuggler had been passed over for promotion by professional officers more connected than he. With that, Arnold found himself here at the Continental Army's headquarters on Bemis Heights above Freeman's Farm reporting to a man who hated him deeply and preferred he not receive a shred of glory or credit for any success on the field of battle. In fact, an officer who had served under Gates was quoted as saying, General Gates despises a certain pompous little fellow.

—⸙⸙⸙—

General Gates ordered the Northern Army to be patient and wait until the British neared before launching a counterattack. General Gates' second in command, American Brigadier General Benedict Arnold, strongly disagreed with Gates' orders, but was forced to remain silent. Arnold was anxious to engage the enemy before they were able to bring up their guns and bombard the American fortifications. The delay in taking a more aggressive approach and ordering an attack would force the Americans to have a painfully negative impact on the battle about to ensue.

Ultimately, not being able to remain silent any longer, Arnold pestered Gates, arguing that he was the man best to lead the troops to prevent the British from breaking through the Rebel lines until Gates finally agreed to give him a limited command with limited responsibility. Gates reluctantly ordered General Arnold along with Colonel Daniel Morgan's corps of riflemen from the First New Hampshire Regiment and Major Henry Dearborn to track the British movements. Both Morgan and Dearborn's light infantry, also of the First, were eager to inflict their revenge from relatively unsuccessful previous engagements at Quebec and Boston. The order was given with the condition that Arnold would receive no reinforcements. If Arnold got into trouble, the only options were for him and his men to fight their way out of it or perish. Secretly, Gates hoped for the latter and that the man he despised would thereby finally be eliminated or, if not so eliminated, be unsuccessful in battle and thus marginalized at the very least.

At about 10:00 am, cannon shots signaled that the British troops were on the move. Burgoyne debouched onto Freeman's Farm in three divisions, Fraser's Advanced Corps on the right, the Germans on the left and he and the remaining British troops in the center.

About 12:30, Morgan's men brushed with the British advance guard and a brief skirmish ensued. Musket fire from Fraser's light infantrymen sent Morgan's men scurrying for cover into the woods. Morgan's men rallied and the New Hampshire Continentals under Arnold's command appeared on the scene for support. With that news, Burgoyne ordered the red coated regulars from the British 21st, 20th, and 62nd divisions to take a position on the northern edge as the Americans under General Enoch Poor finally moved out. In the furious battle that followed, both sides alternately advanced and retreated back and forth for over three hours across the fields of Freeman's Farm, now strewn with bodies. Burgoyne's divisions were barely holding on. Although Arnold was allowed to advance only under the condition that he would not be allowed reinforcements, he recognized that Burgoyne was in a weakened position and that it was time to strike. He ignored the pre-condition and made the request in spite of it. From Gates safely at his desk far back at his headquarters, the request was denied. The troops guarding the Rebel headquarters were to stay in place deeming it not prudent to weaken their position on Bemis Heights. When Gates finally sent General Learned's Brigade later in the day, they were forced back by Fraser's men on the right wing.

The German troops marching along the river road heard the sounds of the escalating battle as they grew closer. Riedesel sent an officer ahead to find out the state of the battle and get further instructions from Burgoyne. Burgoyne ordered the artillery and baggage to be protected while Riedesel was to move as many men as possible in his main force to aid the British center. Just as the British lines began to falter due to the numerically superior American force, German reinforcements arrived from the river road to the east. Attacking the American right, the British line held, and the Americans were forced to withdraw eliminating any hope of an American victory on this day. Despite the late arriving reinforcements, the British troops were shaken by the battle before the arrival of support. They could not advance any further than to a point about a mile north of the American line on the Freeman Farm. There they entrenched and awaited Clinton, who according to plan, was to advance north to Albany from New York City. The Rebels retreated out of the sight of the British in the growing darkness to their encampment on Bemis Heights.

Arnold was upset and frustrated by Gates' reluctance to attack earlier in the battle. He was also disgusted and upset that Gates had refused his request for reinforcements from the safety of his headquarters on Gates Heights, when it was he, Arnold, who was in a position to observe the British weakening and knowing he was in a position to break the enemy. Arnold was confident that striking with reinforcements when he requested them would have yielded a victorious result. He felt that Gates was much more concerned about his own personal safety than he was about winning the battle. Gates was well known for his conservative approach thus gaining him the nickname, Granny Gates. In direct contrast, of course, Arnold was known for his fiery disposition and his aggressive military approach to battle, along with his willingness to physically take the field of battle in leading his troops. He further resented Gates' appointment in charge of the northern command, feeling he had been passed over for the position, one he felt he had earned by his accomplishments in the war to date. To add insult to injury, he found that his name was not even mentioned in Gates' report of the battle to the congress.

He stormed into Gates' headquarters, stood at attention and saluted.

"General Gates, sir, we were defeated in this battle by your failure to strike in a timely fashion," Arnold angrily declared. "He who hesitates has lost! And you cannot lead by sitting behind a desk. An old saw proclaims that you must strike while the anvil is hot, and this far away from the line, by the time you were notified, the anvil had long cooled, and many of our brave soldiers had already been killed by the enemy. And through it all, you hide up here on this hill behind the battle. Why, even your mother knows you cannot push a noodle across a plate, you must pull it!"

His face bright red, Gates replied, "General Arnold, perhaps you have forgotten who is in command here. In the event you have forgotten, I am your direct superior, and I refuse to be preached to by you with your childish sayings, or stand for insubordination by you, or by anyone else for that matter. You are, as of this very moment, relieved of your command!" he shouted, pounding his fist on the desk.

With that said, an enraged Arnold abruptly turned about and stomped out without a salute, or a word said.

—⟨⟨⟨∫∬⟩⟩⟩—

During the fivehour battle, the Americans lost approximately 280 troops while the British suffered a more severe loss of more than 550 men. Without support from the south, along with diminishing supplies, the British army became weaker and weaker with each passing day.

When the din of battle had ceased, the local Saratoga residents waited for some indications of the results. There were no signs of a British retreat since there was no movement north by the troops and the main camp on the Sword farm remained in place. They could only surmise that the battle was not over and that both sides were either taking a respite from the battle to determine their next move or waiting on the other side to make a move. Perhaps one side or the other was waiting for reinforcements. As the days turned to weeks, the residents became increasingly apprehensive, wondering when they might get an indication of what was about to happen and pondering their next personal moves.

In the meantime, the residents could only bide their time until they received some sign of a next move on the part of the British Army or the Continental Army. The British army waited in place for three weeks before Burgoyne was ready to acknowledge that Clinton was not going to arrive in time to help.

CHAPTER 11

S haken by a victory, if indeed it could be called such, since there was no surrender by the enemy and it had come with such a great price, the British army encamped just northwest of the field of battle, southwest of the Great Ravine in the area of the Freeman farm. Burgoyne sent a small contingent to the east along the river to sweep the area. A scouting party identified the empty Schuyler house, abandoned by General Schuyler and his family when the general was notified of the advancing British forces. Having been replaced my General Gates, Schuyler moved his family south to their home in Albany. Burgoyne moved into Schuyler's house, making it his temporary headquarters. There, the British awaited support from Clinton's planned move north to Albany from New York City for nearly three weeks. Meanwhile, a week earlier on September 26th, the British forces under General Howe had occupied Philadelphia forcing the Continental Congress to relocate to York, Pennsylvania.

On October 4th, after two weeks with no new word of Clinton's progress, Burgoyne decided to host a dinner with his generals to discuss strategy and the British army's next moves. The dinner meeting was made possible by the food and supplies left behind by the Schuyler's when they left the house and headed to their Albany home. Some of Dorothy's fall flowers still blooming alongside of the house were used to adorn the table as a centerpiece. Invited to the meeting were Generals Fraser, Hamilton and von Riedesel, accompanied by their wives, to discuss their options. Burgoyne also invited and introduced Abigail Simpson, the now widowed wife of Captain William Simpson, a woman he had gotten to know very well over the last several months.

Standing, with wine glasses held aloft, Burgoyne followed the toast before the meal by saying, "I would like to introduce Mrs. Abigail Simpson to you. She has most recently lost her husband at Bennington where he served the crown with courage, dignity, and honor."

"On behalf of we here, in addition to all who served under your courageous husband, may I extend our condolences for your loss and our appreciation for his exemplary service," added General Hamilton.

"Thank you," she replied humbly with head bowed. The other three women smiled politely. Riedesel's wife could hardly keep silent with the disgust she held for what she considered the total lack of morality of the British officers that she had observed during the campaign.

"Well, gentlemen, here are our options as I see them. I invite your opinions and please introduce any other approach of which I am not aware," Burgoyne began. "I am open to all suggestions to approaches for what lies ahead, but when I make the call, we move forward as one. Do we all agree?"

All the officers present nodded their heads in agreement.

As he saw it, the British had three choices. Two of the choices involved moving ahead with their drive to Albany in one of two ways. Burgoyne's heavily burdened army had either to make a run through the narrow passage between the hills and the river, risking total destruction, or drive the Americans out of their fortifications on Bemis Heights. The third was to stay put or retreat to a point where they felt it safe to wait for word from Clinton as to when the planned reinforcements from the south would arrive.

"My biggest concern right now is that we are not fully aware of the Rebels' position. If our advance is too slow, or from the wrong direction, our limited supplies could be open to attack," Hamilton offered.

Riedesel, in stilted English, expressed his desire to wait for word from the southern contingent. "To not wait for reinforcement holds much risk. In addition, we are facing desertions while the Rebels' numbers are growing. I believe we should retreat to the north to our earlier position where we can still communicate with our supply lines and reinforcements to the north and wait for General Clinton's troops."

"We should have heard from General Clinton by now." offered Fraser. "If the floating bridge we constructed across the Hudson should fall into Rebel hands, we will have no escape route and will be forced to surrender. I would like to hear what General Burgoyne proposes."

"At this point we shall not retreat," Burgoyne declared. "We shall leave eight hundred men to defend our boats and supplies by the river. We shall send a reconnaissance force of 1,500 men to determine the Rebel position and strength. If we determine the Rebels are vulnerable and can be attacked successfully, we will immediately attack with General Fraser's troops on the right, General Riedesel's from the left, and General Hamilton down the center. Only if it is determined we are at too great a disadvantage shall we retreat to Batten Kill and await General Clinton's arrival."

After an after-dinner aperitif, the guests, with the exception of Mrs. Simpson, were on their way out the door to return to their quarters. Mrs. Riedesel looked down her nose at Abigail Simpson as she exited. Then Mrs. Riedesel coyly asked, "Can we accompany you safely to your destination?"

Red faced and awkwardly stumbling for words, Mrs. Simpson replied, "Thank you, but I have made other arrangements as I have a personal issue to discuss with the general."

Shortly after the officers and their wives exited, the guards posted around the house watched all the windows go dark except those in the main bedroom from whence they could hear female giggling followed by male laughter.

Having decided on October 4th to attack the Rebels, a reconnaissance force was to be sent out first to check out the Rebel position and to determine its strength. Three days later, early in the morning, a reconnaissance force of about 1500 men set out in three columns as planned. If the report was positive, as hoped, the British light infantry would take the right, while a detachment of Brunswickers would take the center, and British grenadiers would take the left flank. Fraser and his men were to take a long route west with some Indians, Loyalists, and Canadians in an attempt to divert the Rebels.

Not yet fully aware of the Rebels' position, on the 6th of October, Fraser, remembering that the young Emerson who had scouted and advised of the best approach to Ticonderoga was from this area, General Fraser sought him out. He asked his adjutant to bring Emerson to him.

"Being from these parts, how well do you know this area?" Fraser queried the young Loyalist.

"Pretty well, but not as well as my friend, Philip Eames, who is a long-hunter and is very familiar with this whole area better than anyone I know," replied Emerson.

"Is he with us? Would he help us?"

"Yes, sir. I am sure he would. His father served under you in the French and Indian War and remained in the colonies after his enlistment. We have spoken about it often."

"Then, dispatch him and ask him to report his findings directly to me."

———

Along with the adjutant, Emerson arrived at Philip's and Renee's door. Before Michael could speak, the adjutant knocked on the door, and ordered in a loud voice, "General Fraser of his majesty's colonial forces demands your service."

Philip immediately took Renee by the arm and moved her and the baby to the bedroom at the rear of the little farmhouse. He reached for his rifle and leaned his back against the wall to one side of the door.

"Back up ten paces and drop your weapons," he demanded. He slid along the wall and peered out the window.

He could see that they had not complied.

"Philip, it's me, Michael. There is no threat. I just thought you might be able to help us. Can you come out?"

"Who is that with you? I will not be spoken to in that manner. You know me better than that."

"We are backing up, Philip. Please come out."

From the window Philip could see that they had complied. He slowly opened the door, keeping his weapon ready as he motioned to the soldier to drop his weapon. The soldier, appearing somewhat disgusted, reluctantly complied.

Philip stepped out of the house with his loaded rifle resting on his hip pointing toward the sky. Michael explained the situation and asked Philip if he would scout the colonial rebel army's position. Philip thought for several moments. Unaware to Michael, he still had not decided on his position regarding the conflict. He tried to remain neutral for as long as possible, but apparently his time had run out. He thought of Drew's words. Suddenly he realized how much he had at stake and that he must make the decision best for his family. He must protect them at all costs.

"Philip, General Fraser's forces are camped on Freeman's farm. The rebels are camped somewhere to the south. We need your help to find their camp. You know the area better than anyone else. Will you help us?"

"First of all, Michael, your friend here does not have a manner that inspires cooperation."

"I am sorry, sir," replied the sergeant, hands on hips and a friendlier expression on his face. "It has been a stressful year."

Several thoughts rushed through Philip's mind. He must not reveal his indecision. He must be sure, above all, that now that the war had reached Saratoga, he must do everything possible to guarantee the safety of Renee and his son.

"I have a son now, Michael. I cannot leave my home now that the war is at my door. I must protect Renee and my son."

"I will speak to General Fraser," offered the sergeant. "I am his adjutant, and I can assure you that, if you help us, he will guarantee the safety of your family. I am sure he will assign men to guard your home and family."

"In that case, I will locate the colonial forces for you, but since this task must be done on foot, you must follow me to Bemis Tavern and return my horse here."

"I will accompany you and bring your horse back here. When you get to the British camp, I will escort you to the general's headquarters so you can report their position to him. I am sure he will want to meet you and thank you personally," replied Michael.

"Give me a moment," Philip said as he lowered his musket, turned, and entered the cabin to inform Renee of the plan. The soldier retrieved his weapon, and Philip returned with a bedroll, a supply of beef jerky, bread, and a canteen of water.

"Where is the British camp?" he asked.

"Just north of the Great Ravine on the south end of the Sword farm," replied Michael. "The Rebels withdrew south of the Freeman farm a couple of weeks ago."

"I may need some time, but hopefully I will make it back to your camp by late in the day."

"When you are confronted by British sentries north of the Freeman farm, inform them of who you are. They will be aware of your mission and your name. They will escort you to General Fraser."

Philip fetched his horse and secured his bedroll and supplies behind the saddle. The men mounted their horses and headed south in the direction of Bemis Heights. About a mile south behind the Bemis Tavern, Philip unloaded his supplies from his horse and handed the reins to Michael.

"Michael, promise me that my home and family will be protected. Give me your word that your superior officers understand that I am doing this only on this condition. I am taking you at your word."

"Philip, you have my word."

"Sir, you do not know me, but I am a man of honor, and you have my word as well," added the sergeant.

Michael and Philip embraced, and Philip and the soldier shook hands. Philip entered the forest and began to make his way north on foot shielded from visibility by the foliage on the trees and the underbrush. Accompanied by the sergeant, Michael mounted his horse and, with Philip's horse in tow, headed north along the river road. He and the British soldier would return Philip's horse to his farm and then report back to General Fraser.

After proceeding about a quarter of a mile, Philip could see colonial infantrymen and cannons which he surmised were the reason the British were forced to move west instead of advancing directly south to where the battle of two weeks earlier took place. Proceeding along the base of The Heights, he was able to identify the Rebel position above him. Staying under cover of the trees and underbrush, he surveyed as much of the Rebel position as he could without being observed. After completing his task, he headed north for about a half mile and then northwest along the Mill Creek towards a point where he knew he could ford the creek, west-to-east at a low point. He then proceeded northeast until he could see the tents revealing the location of the British camp. He approached the tents undetected until reaching a clearing at the edge of the camp. The sentries posted at the southern edge of the camp were expecting him, and one the sentries left his post to escort him directly to General Fraser's headquarters. The sentry entered the general's tent, and within a couple of moments exited. He asked Philip to remain where he was standing, in front of the general's tent, and headed towards the tents of the British soldiers directly in front of the general's tent, but several yards away.

Philip paced back and forth in front of the two guards standing on each side of the entrance to General Fraser's tent.

Within minutes, the sentry returned with Michael Emerson.

"Philip!" Michael exclaimed with a smile signifying his pleasure in reuniting with his old friend.

"Michael!" Philip returned as the two men embraced. He observed the general over Michael's shoulder as General Fraser lifted the flaps of his tent, exited, and stood just outside of the entrance. Less tense now than at their brief meeting at his farm a few hours earlier, Philip remarked with a smile, 'I didn't mention it before, but you look well. Military life agrees with you."

"You look well also. I'm so glad you were able to help. The adjutant expressed your concerns to General Fraser,"

"Gentlemen," Fraser started without emotion, as he stepped out of his tent. "Shall we get to the business at hand?"

"Yes sir, General, sir," Michael replied as he turned to introduce his friend to the general, as the smile fell from his face. "General Fraser, sir, this is Philip Eames, the man of whom I spoke to you about.... the long-hunter, the scout?"

"Sir," Philip said, bowing his head slightly, not really knowing what the proper way to address a military officer of such high rank would be.

"Yes. Eames, your friend speaks highly of you, your loyalty, and your father's service to the king in the French and Indian conflict. Thank you for helping us."

"Yes, sir. It is an honor and a pleasure. I did however ask for a favor in return."

"I see. Please refresh my memory."

"My property, my wife, and my child. I asked that they be spared by the soldiers and the Indians."

"Oh yes, yes, of course.......of course. My adjutant spoke to me in that regard. I apologize. You should not have had to ask. The king's soldiers are trained to respect the dignity of all loyal subjects of The Crown."

"Yes, sir, I have always believed that, but we have heard a great deal about........."

"Yes, yes, I am aware......the Indians.....Jane McCrea," interrupted Fraser. "A very unfortunate thing, but I promise we will take special

precautions to ensure that your family and property is not harmed.........
not by anyone. Now what did you find out about the location of the
Rebels."

"Well, they are camped on Bemis Heights, just north of the tavern,
south of Freemen's Farm, about one and a half kilometers southwest
from here. It appears they are using the Nielson house as their general's
headquarters. Their right occupies the summit of a hill by the river road.
It is a position which provides a good command of the road which they
have blocked with a contingent of troops. The camp forms an arc of a
circle with the convex side facing your position. Just below the heights
runs a heavily wooded ravine. The ground runs level from the bottom of
the ravine to their left until it meets a knoll. Parts of this level terrain are
cleared, and other parts are covered with felled trees. In front of this level
area are several small fields from left to right that drops off by the river
road. This whole area is populated with breastworks, but not trenches.
Penetration on the left is almost impossible and exceedingly difficult on
the right. Beyond that area in the direction of your camp are the open
farm fields, wooded on each side at higher elevations. Of course, you are
already well aware of this area which is part of the Freeman Farm. You
are also familiar with the ravines, two running east-west and the third
perpendicular to them at somewhat of a right angle to the river. As you
well know, the bottom of the great ravine is a soft bog populated with
brush. Michael knows it well. He could lead an advance scouting party."

Philip turned to Michael.

"But I suggest such a party use the protection of the woods. As you
might imagine, from Bemis Heights they will have great command of the
field if you get too close, and a greater visibility of your approach from
their right than you have from any point." Michael nodded agreement.

"How about their strength.....their numbers?" asked the general.

"I am not skilled at estimating such, and I would say from the
ground it is almost impossible for anyone to determine who has the edge
in terms of numbers."

"Do we have enough intelligence, Emerson? Any other questions
for your friend?"

"No, Sir," answered Michael. "I am familiar with the area."

"Very good, then. Eames, I ask you to consider joining our militia and serve the king as did your father. We will put your talents to good use."

"Yes, sir, I will do so once I feel assured that my family and property are safe."

"Sir, I would be glad to stand guard at the Eames farm," offered Michael.

"Thank you for volunteering, Emerson. However, I believe it is important that the post be filled by someone in a British uniform. That in itself should be enough to notify our men that the Eames property is off limits and to ward off any natives who might have other ideas. Private Smiley has already been informed of the assignment. I would ask that you escort him to the Eames farm as soon as possible tomorrow."

"Yes, sir," Michael responded.

Philip knew that dusk would be quickly approaching and that he would not be able to reach his farm from the location of the British camp before darkness fell. He nodded his head toward Fraser in a slight bow, embraced Michael once more, and took his leave, heading into the woods. He would camp overnight in the forest when he could no longer find his way due to darkness and ultimately head in the direction of the river road in the morning. His intent was to find a place to spend the night in the forest while he still had time to make camp and gather some wood for a fire. Michael left headed towards the soldiers' tents in search of Private Smiley. Fraser set out for General Burgoyne's tent to inform him of what he had found from Philip regarding the location of the Rebel's camp.

━━◅◍▻━━

Philip emerged from the forest south of the Pearson's store just as dawn was breaking. As he approached the Pearson's store, something appeared different. It took a few moments for his brain to determine just what it was. Then, as he started to climb the steps, it occurred to him. The door was closed! It was only on frigid winter days that the door was normally closed if the store was open for business, and the temperature this day was quite comfortable. Philip reached for the door handle and was met with resistance.

The door was locked! He hesitated for a moment. Baffled, he knocked. After a few moments, he knocked again, this time harder. Finally, he decided that perhaps Martha and her father were still in the living quarters above the store because something had happened to one or both of them. There was an entrance to the stairs leading upstairs from the store on the ground floor, but the entrance directly to the stairs to the living quarters was through a door on the dock in the rear of the store. He rushed to the rear of the store, climbed the stairs to the dock and knocked on the living quarter's door. Still no answer! He called Martha's name and knocked again, harder. After several tries, frustrated, he returned to the main store entrance at the front and knocked again, calling Martha by name. He finally could hear footsteps, and momentarily the door opened. Martha rushed to him, burying her head in his chest. Instinctively, he embraced her, but said nothing. She was sobbing, and without looking up, uttered through her tears, "Philip, Papa is dead."

"What happened?" he forced out, his voice trembling.

Martha, still sobbing, described the events of the early morning. Burying her head again in Philip's chest, he held her until she slowly lifted her head and dried her eyes on her sleeve.

—◦◦◦—

The previous evening was as any evening, dinner followed by some conversation with her father about the day's business, plans for the next day, a piece of pie and some tea or some wine, reading if not too tired, and then to bed.

As one entered the store, the counter was to the left, and a fireplace on the opposite wall. The cooking for meals was done on a stove on the ground floor along the back wall of the store in order not to have to haul firewood up the narrow stairs. Upstairs over the store were the sleeping quarters housing two bedrooms. Grates in the ceiling above the two stoves, the one at the back of the store principally for cooking and the Franklin stove in the center for heating, allowed the heat to rise into the bedrooms above. The table used for dining was located within just a few feet from the cooking stove.

On that evening at about 8:30, Sam Pearson rose from the table. After a long day, he was ready for bed. As he headed for the stairs leading to the sleeping quarters, carrying the lantern from the center of the table to light the way, he called out to Martha over his shoulder.

"Martha, can you bolt the door for me? I'm especially tired this evening."

"Yes, Papa," Martha replied as she headed towards the door......... "Good night."

She lit a wooden splint from the fireplace fire and then lit a candle with it that she placed on the end of the counter closest to the door. Then she proceeded to the door, and just as she was lifting the iron bar Drew had provided to lower it into its horizontal position to prevent entry, the door burst open with a force from the other side that thrust Martha backwards with a start. Screaming, she fell to the floor landing on her back. Sam Pearson had already taken a few steps up the stairs when he heard the noise from the door, Martha's screaming, and her body hitting the floor. His heart seemed to stop for a moment, and then pounded so loudly that not only could he feel it, but he thought he could hear it. He reversed his steps instinctively and descended the stairs. As he came through the door, the lantern still in his hand, he turned to the corner by the door to retrieve the loaded musket he kept there each night. Suddenly a shot rang out and Sam Pearson fell to the floor as the lantern skidded across the floor, flickered, and went out.

A giant of a man with a kerchief across his face ordered, "Get up, wench!" At the same time, he reached down with his right hand, the left hand still holding the weapon he had just fired, and grabbing her arm, pulled her up towards him. As Martha struggled to her feet, the intruder grabbed her around her waist from behind. He pushed her toward the counter and pressed her against it, placing his spent musket on the counter with one hand as he pressed her head against the counter face down with the other. As he held her head down, with the other hand he lifted her skirt and shift to her waist providing him access to her bare buttocks. Then, as he leaned back and reached to his waist to loosen his belt and lower his pants with his free hand, his hold on Martha lightened. Silent through all this, Martha, feeling the diminished pressure, thrust herself backwards sending the man backward to the floor, landing on his backside with she on top of him.

This gave Martha the time she needed to get to her knees, to crawl behind the counter, and to retrieve the loaded pistol always kept there. For several seconds there was no sound except for the man's heavy breathing breaking the silence. The only light was from the candle on the counter, the light from the fireplace, and the moonlight through the window casting a strip of light across the floor. This was not the first time she had to find her way around the store in semi-darkness. As the moonlight streaming through the window revealed her assailant still sprawled on his back, Martha shouted, "I have a loaded pistol and I can see you!"

The intruder rose to his knees quickly, moved from the revealing strip of moonlight, and crawled to the counter, reaching over it to retrieve his rifle. Rising to his feet, realizing that he was in a vulnerable position not being able to clearly discern anything or anyone in the semi-darkness, he scurried out the door. Martha waited several minutes without moving or making a sound. Then, hearing nothing and feeling assured her assailant was no longer in the store, she found her way to the door and dropped the metal bar into place. Finding her way back to the counter to retrieve the candle, and then holding it above her head, she was able to find her father's lifeless form. Rushing to her father's side, she sank to her knees and placed the candle on the floor beside him. She lowered her ear to her father's mouth. Sam Pearson was not breathing!

"Papa, Papa, no, no," she cried, lifting his head and holding it to her breast. She held him for what seemingly to her was only moments, oblivious to all around her, sobbing until, exhausted from the ordeal, she fell asleep on his chest until she was awakened by Philip pounding on the door just as the sun was rising.

"Philip, what shall we do?" Philip was torn by a desire to return to Renee and a compulsion to pursue Sam Pearson's killer before he had time to get far out of reach.

"First, I must catch up with him, the one who did this.

I will find him, and he shall pay."

"But what about the British? There surely will be more trouble, more fighting. Renee and Robert will be in danger."

"I have spoken to a British general. He has sent soldiers by now to guard Renee and Robert. I will tell you more about this later, but now I must go now before the scoundrel gets too far ahead of me. I must get word to Renee that I must do this, and that I will be gone for a short time. It should not take long for me to catch up with him and take care of this if I go now!"

"Yes, Jotham Bemis should be in soon. This is the morning he normally comes in for supplies. He will pass right by your place on his way back to the tavern."

Jotham was the proprietor of the Bemis Tavern and farm a few miles south of Philip's homestead, just to the south of Bemis Heights. Renee would be fine, Philip felt, accepting the word of General Fraser as an officer and a gentleman. She was quite used to his being away on long hunting and trapping trips, and this time the British army would be there to protect her. Philip thought that Soldat would be a big help in finding the perpetrator's trail but knew the dog would give a warning to Renee and a British guard should a stranger approach. Also, he obviously did not want to take the time to retrieve him. He concluded that his tracking and stalking skills, mastered over the years as a trapper, would serve him well enough.

After examining the fresh boot and horse tracks beside the store entrance, he determined that a horse had been chased off and that a man had proceeded into the woods on foot via the southeast path. This was a path that he himself had used before and with which he was quite familiar. With this person having an hour or two's lead on him, and with a full day of light ahead of him, it would probably be close to dusk before the man would rest from his escape and make camp for the night. He took some provisions from the store and began the slow and arduous process of tracking the scoundrel down. He thought it might not take long to catch up with him if the killer stayed on the trail.

Philip was able to stay on the trail for perhaps a mile before it thinned out and disappeared from lack of use. From there, by using his tracking skills, he could see that the imposter's path continued in a southwesterly direction. His search through the woods continued for another half hour when he suddenly detected a faint smell of smoke. Following the scent, it became stronger and stronger, until by climbing a tree he could see a small clearing where a man was leaning forward reclining on a fallen tree, eating. Obviously, the man had not waited until dusk to stop, but decided that he was safe enough to stop to partake of some sustenance. Philip quietly moved from tree to tree in a hunched position until he was within five to ten yards from him.

He stepped into the open, and with his body partly blocked by a tree, pistol in his left hand, a tomahawk in his right, Philip commanded; "Raise your hands above your head."

The man was startled! Big Will rose and turned into full view, drawing his pistol from his waist with his right hand, moving to cock the hammer with his left. Before Will could draw the hammer of the pistol back, Philip raised his tomahawk over his head with his right hand and falling to his left knee, launched it forward with full force towards its target. Before Philip could switch his pistol to his right hand from his left and cock the hammer, the tomahawk had reached its target firmly in the center of Big Will Stanton's chest. Will's pistol fired wildly as he fell to the ground on his back. Philip approached the body cautiously and could see as he stood at the man's feet that Will Stanton was dead. Stunned, he could not believe what he had just done.

How would his God judge him? What would his Quaker mother have thought of him?

Suddenly, coming to his senses, with his heart pounding he scratched out a shallow grave. Unsure that the grave would protect Will's body from scavenging animals, he feverishly covered the site with stones. He knew he would return for Will to bring him out of the woods for a proper burial. As he prepared the grave, Philip wondered to himself why he had drawn the tomahawk and used it instead of his pistol. Although he had never used his tomahawk on a man, his thought was that his instincts must have dictated that he preferred it from his using it so often for chopping wood for a fire or to construct a lean-to as a long-hunter. He seldom used a pistol except perhaps occasionally from short range to finish off a buck he had shot with his rifle. He thought that luck surely had something to do with it reaching its target in that the only times he had ever thrown it that far was to pass the time of day during idol times by attempting to hit a tree to entertain himself.

As he returned to the store, he thought that Will's family would have to be notified, but then recalled that his only family, his parents, had passed some time ago. When he reached the store, he told Martha what had happened back in the woods.

"I will need to report this to the sheriff and the constable. I am somewhat concerned as to whether they will believe my story."

"I am sure they will believe your story along with mine. They know your reputation, and have no fear, you shall not be detained. "

"Martha, regardless of the law or the justification of my actions, I shall never be free from what I have done. I am not God, yet I have acted as such. I have never killed a man, nor did I ever intend to under any circumstances."

"Philip, do not admonish yourself. You had no choice but to defend yourself."

"Lord, God, forgive me," Philip spoke softly, bringing his hand to his forehead, staring at the floor. Then, still not completely coming to his senses, he continued in short cryptic sentences; "You must contact Ebenezer. He will bring your father to the preacher. Drew will build a casket. We will have a fine service for your father."

He was sure that a modest, but respectful service for Martha's father would be performed at the church. Being well known as proprietor of perhaps the only general store in the North Country, he was sure that people would want to come to pay their respects from miles around.

After a few moments of silence, Philip asked; "What will become of the store? Surely you cannot carry it on alone!" Philip responded nervously.

"I am sure Ebenezer will help me run it. Please, do not worry," she responded.

Ebenezer Storm was Sam Pearson's best, if not his only friend. He had lost his wife to the same disease as Sam had lost his a few years earlier and would spend time with Sam fishing on a Sunday afternoon from time to time.

"But this is not the time to concern yourself about this. You must go to Renee."

"Yes, yes......... Of course."

Philip placed both hands on Martha's shoulders and looked directly into her eyes.

"I cannot explain just now how I know of such, but there soon will be another battle, almost exactly where the one of three weeks ago occurred. I must make sure that Renee and my son are safe. Lock your doors. If anyone approaches, hide in the cellar, I will come back for you as soon as I can."

"Philip, go quickly. I will be safe. In addition to the fact that I am a woman, neither side will destroy the only source of supplies that they both need."

"Do not be so sure. Please do as I say. Either side would be desirous of taking control of the store. I must go."

"Yes, please, just go. Take Papa's horse. I will be fine."

"Thank you. .....Yes, I will need a horse," Philip replied as if suddenly returning to reality from a trance.

He quickly ran to the stable, and glancing back at Martha, mounted Sam's horse and urged him in the direction of his farm without looking back.

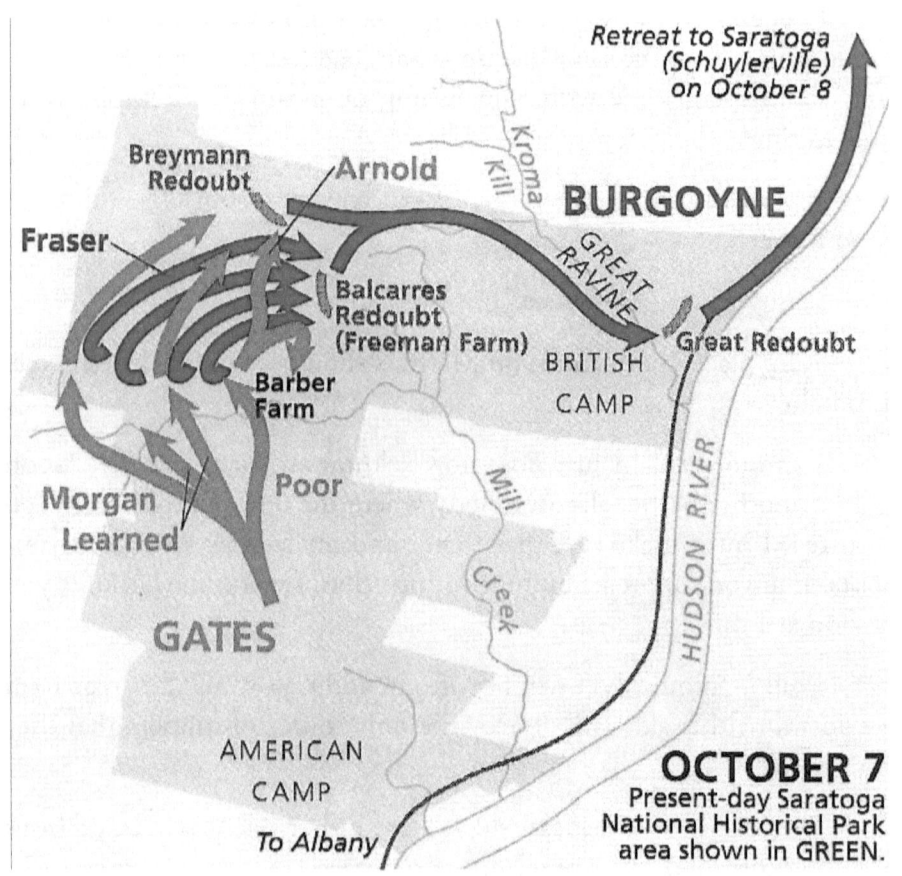

Saratoga National Historical Park Visitor's Guide

CHAPTER 12

On that same morning of October 7th, as Philip was heading out of the woods toward the Pearson's, the 1,500-man force supported by eight cannons moved south out of the British camp in three columns. The British light infantry deployed on the right. A detachment of Brunswickers and jagers took the center, and the British grenadiers took the left. Fraser's force, including, along with his men, Loyalists, Canadians, and Indians, headed west to divert the Rebels. The plan was for the troops to march southwestwardly about three miles to a clearing on the Barber Farm.

The British had constructed three redoubts just north of the Barber Farm. A redoubt was a structure formed from logs with one end sharpened to a point in a spear-like fashion. The unsharpened ends of the logs were buried in an arc shaped earthen berm exposing approximately four feet of the logs at about a 45-degree angle with the ground with the pointed ends facing outward. This sort of makeshift fort was used for defending a military headquarters, backup forces, or for protection by a retreating force against an advancing enemy.

The Great Redoubt was close to the river, originally intended to protect the high ground and river flats where the army's artillery, supplies, hospital and bateau were stationed. A second redoubt known as the Breymann Redoubt under the command of Lieutenant Colonel Breymann was about four miles to the west. The third redoubt, known as the Balcarres Redoubt, under General Alexander Lindsay, the 6th

Earl of Balcarres, was a few hundred yards northwest of the Breymann Redoubt. Both the Breymann and Balcarres Redoubts faced in a westward direction.

The British troops advanced to a clearing on the Barber Farm in open fields spread over a wide area, rendering both flanks vulnerable to a surprise attack from woods on their flanks. The troops were segregated into three columns. The column to the Rebel's left would be commanded by General Simon Fraser whose unit was composed of his nephew's advance party, Major Lord Balcarres's light infantry, and the 24th regiment. Balcarres would also take command of his redoubt if needed. British grenadiers made up the column on the enemy's right under Major John Acland.

Both British flanks rested against the woods, under the cover from which they could be attacked. The right was also skirted by a high vantage point from which the Rebels could command a view of their adversary's position. The cover of the woods gave the Patriots the advantage of fighting in a way that suited them. Morgan was in his element, and Poor had been quick to learn to use the forest to his advantage. The battle on the flanks would be on the American Patriot's terms.

The center would be under the command of General von Riedesel with soldiers from all the Brunswick units plus the German jagers and about five hundred men under Lieutenant Colonel Breymann in his redoubt. Burgoyne would back up the columns with the remainder of the British troops from their headquarters to the east.

Hardly three quarters of a mile into the march, just south of Freeman's Farm, Burgoyne, Philips, and Riedesel, in an attempt to spot the Americans with a telescope, climbed atop the roof of a log cabin. They could see nothing but trees which concealed an American officer accompanied by a scout from view within a thousand yards of their position. An American officer and scout had been deployed to check out an earlier report by pickets that the British troops were on the move. Ironically, it was the Americans that spotted the British generals instead, in full display atop the cabin.

As the Americans were about to return to their headquarters to report their findings, they heard horses approaching. Taking cover in the woods, they remained in hiding as two men, a British soldier accompanied by another rider not dressed in uniform, came within sight just a few yards away. Seeing the British soldier, the Rebel officer and the scout raised their rifles and fired when the two riders were within ten yards of them. Michael Emerson and Private Smiley, on their way to the Eames farm, slumped over and fell from their saddles to the ground, both dead. Minutes later the sound of British cannon echoed throughout the ravines. Within 15 minutes of observing Burgoyne and company, the officer and the scout notified General Gates of their discovery.

Taking note of this vital information reported by the officer and the scout, Gates ordered John Wilkinson, a senior officer, to investigate. Under cover of the forest, Wilkinson reached a point where he could observe the British forces from a distance of about 1,000 feet. What he saw was the redcoats sitting in formation in the wheat field with their firearms between their legs. He returned to headquarters on Bemis Heights and reported his findings to Gates. He described the British position as resting between woods on both eastern and western sides, from which they could be approached unseen. His advice to Gates was to attack.

"I think, sir, they offer you battle."

"Well, then, order on Morgan to begin the game."

News of Wilkinson's findings circulated throughout headquarters. Although Benedict Arnold had been relieved of his command, he stayed in camp hanging on. When the sound of gunfire could be heard in the distance, he was convinced the pickets were under attack. He immediately decided he must confront Gates once again and express contrition for his remarks. With feigned remorse, he entered Gates' quarters with hat in hand. Arnold requested permission to simply go out to the lines to observe what was happening with the promise to return with a more detailed account. Gates hesitated, bringing his hand under his chin.

"Frankly, I am afraid to trust you, Arnold."

Major General Arnold promised to not give any commands in the commander's name even if he felt the pickets needed support. Gates reluctantly agreed but sent General Lincoln along with him just as a precaution. As drums were beating to arms, the two generals mounted their steeds and cantered off toward the sound of gunfire in the distance. Within thirty minutes, they returned with the news that the enemy was on the move, threatening the army's left flank. Lincoln confirmed Arnold's observations, adding that, without reinforcements, Morgan's company was in danger of being decimated.

"Well, we will have Morgan and company make a wide swing to the left in order to outflank them."

With an ice-cold look, Arnold retorted sharply, "That is nothing. You must send a strong force."

"General Arnold, frankly, I have nothing for you to do. You have no further business here."

It was not that Arnold's conclusion was invalid, but his demeanor had resulted in his crossing the line once again. Benedict Arnold had lost his opportunity to take part in the ensuing battle for a second time. As Gates' anger cooled and the redness receded from his face, Lincoln stepped up. The more restrained General Lincoln interceded and was able to convince Gates to commit to supporting Morgan. As a result, Poor's Brigade was ordered to attack the left of the British line while Morgan was ordered to circle around their right. The plan was that the two brigades would move stealthily through the woods and attack the enemy from both sides at the same moment. Learned's brigade would remain in reserve waiting to attack from the center at the same time that the British forces were attacked from both flanks.

"Well then, order Morgan to begin the game!" Ordered Gates.

The Bemis Tavern, just below Bemis Heights, provided Sally Bemis with the opportunity to observe an early indication that the battle that had occurred earlier in September was about to resume. Fewer and fewer rebel soldiers were frequenting the tavern. She suspected that something was about to happen but did not react immediately. When she suddenly heard British cannons echoing throughout the Great Ravine on that early October day, breaking the deafening three-week silence from the sounds of combat, a chill suddenly came over her. Her thoughts at once went to Drew Gerard as she stood at a table in the tavern taking an order from patrons. She was momentarily paralyzed, but then impulsively ripped off her apron and ran from the tavern. Feverishly, she hitched a horse to her father's buggy, and without announcing to anyone what she was about to do, climbed into the buggy and urged the horse into a gallop up the river road toward Drew's home and black smiting barn. About halfway there, as she approached a slight left hand turn at too high a speed, the buggy hit a rut on the right side of the road, sending the buggy off in the same direction, and ripping the right rear wheel from its frame. Struggling to hang on, the tomboy in Sally Bemis served her well, enabling her to gain control of the horse and the buggy and bring the horse to a halt. She quickly unharnessed the horse and, hiking up her dress, mounted the horse bareback. She continued her mission at a gallop toward Drew's quarters as adeptly as any man in the same situation. Arriving at Drew's barn, she dismounted quickly.

"Drew, Drew!" She shouted as she ran towards the man with whom she had fallen in love. As Drew appeared at the door of the barn, she threw herself into his arms at such a force, he was forced to brace himself quickly so as not to not fall backwards.

He held her as she buried her head into his chest, quieting her as he stroked her back.

"Shhhh, shhhhh ...what is it?"

"The British.......the American troops....on The Heights....cannon fire," she gasped!

She went on to further describe the decreasing activity at the tavern she had seen over the past several weeks, and how the cannon fire she had heard had caused her to panic.

"Stay here. You will be safe here. Both sides need the only smith in the area. I must go to Philip and Renee."

He ripped his leather apron from his waist, dropping it on the ground and snatching his rifle from the corner as he ran, he quickly saddled his horse. Without any further words, he took Sally in his arms, kissed her deeply, turned, mounted his horse, and galloped down the path onto the river road towards Philip and Renee's farm. On the way, he stopped at the Pearsons to warn them to take cover in the cellar. He met Martha at the door of the store, but thought nothing of Sam Pearson's absence, assuming he was at work in the back room.

With the sounds of battle in the background, Drew arrived at the Eames farm and knocked on the door.

" Renee, it's me. Drew."

"Come in. Come in. What is happening?"

"The battle is not over! Where is Philip?" He exclaimed as he rushed in looking left and right for Philip.

"The day before yesterday, Michael Emerson and a British soldier came to the door and asked him to find the location of the colonial patriot's headquarters. Philip said that he would if the British would ensure our safety. They agreed and Philip left with them. He said he would return today, but then a terrible thing happened. Mr. Bemis stopped by this morning on his return from Pearson's and said that Mr. Pearson had been killed. He said Philip is searching for his killer in the forest."

Drew's face dropped from shock and surprise to a deep frown.

"My God!" Drew responded, his shock reflected in his voice. He took the rifle that Philip had left for Renee from the corner and leaned it against the wall next to the window to the left of the door. Then he went to the window to the right of the door with his musket by his side, "Tend to Robert. I will stand watch from the window. I will summon you if I need your assistance."

Within minutes Drew observed two Indians coming up the path to the house.

"Renee, go to that window. The musket is ready. The intruders are here," he commanded, pointing to the window to the left of the door. She lowered Robert to the floor and rushed to her post.

One Indian approached the door and banged on it hard. Drew turned to Renee and brought his forefinger to his lips signaling Renee to remain quiet. There was a look of horror on her face. When there was no response, the Indian backed away and joined the other just staring at the house. Drew and Renee exchanged glances pensively, wondering what the Indians were planning to do. A smell of smoke rose in the air. Then a torch crashed through the window of the bedroom at the rear of the house. The house filled with smoke, and Drew knew they could not remain inside the burning structure much longer. They would surely be asphyxiated or burned to death if they chose to remain.

Drew smashed the window he was guarding and fired his musket at the Indian closest to him. The Indian fell forward, dead. The other Indian, startled, sought cover behind a nearby tree. An Indian warrior at the rear of the house came around the side of the house and appeared briefly before he also took cover behind a tree. Drew knew they were trapped. He ran to the other window with his musket in his right hand and retrieved the other from Renee with his left.

"Take Robert and follow me. I will keep them busy long enough for you to make it to the woods."

Drew raised both rifles to his waist, one in each hand, and kicked open the door. As he exited, both Indians emerged from the protection of their respective trees. Before they could brace themselves squarely into a position to fire, Drew braced the muskets on his thighs, pointed them at the savage closest to his right side and fired at him, hitting him squarely in his chest. As his target fell to the ground, he turned to face the Indian at his left.

"Run, Renee, run!" He shouted.

Before he could get his second shot off, the Indian to his left raised and fired his weapon, striking Drew directly in the chest. Drew looked down at his wound with a bewildered expression and toppled forward face first on the ground dead! Renee was already running alongside of the house into the woods. Soldat, who had been observing the scene confused, but with his haunches lowered in an attack position, followed her. Suddenly she tripped on the underbrush and then her skirt, releasing Robert to the ground in order to steady herself. She rolled over into a sitting position, startled, looking up at the Indian now hovering over her.

Soldat was facing the Indian growling, lips curled, teeth showing, saliva dripping from his tongue, and the hair raised on the back of his neck. The Indian struck Soldat with the butt of his musket, and the dog went rolling to the side, semiconscious. The savage reached down, and grabbing Renee by her hair, pulled her forward. He dragged her shrieking, face down to the front of the house and shoved her face first into the earth. He climbed on her back, drew his tomahawk from his waist, raised it into the air and buried it squarely into her back. Renee lay dead as he took his knife and circled her head with the blade cutting skin deep from her forehead to the nape of her neck and then back from the other side. He raised himself, placing a knee on her back as he leaned forward, and with a loud blood curdling cry, using both hands, ripped her hair from her scalp. He then proceeded to scalp Drew in the same manner. Raising himself to a standing position with his trophies in hand, he walked away down the path in the direction from whence he came.

At about 3:30 in the afternoon, the Americans were ordered to attack in three columns under Colonel Daniel Morgan on the left, General Enoch Poor on the right, and General Ebenezer Learned in the center. Once the Rebel troops were dispatched, Arnold mounted his horse, and followed the troops. When the troops were in place, awaiting orders, he lingered along the edge of the forest to the west of the field in anticipation of the ensuing battle.

As the British troops were beginning to advance, Poor, hidden by the forest, was unobserved by the British left as well as was Morgan hidden by the forest from General Fraser on the British right. Poor's assault on the British left wounded Major Acland leaving his column with no leadership or artillery support. His grenadiers, still firing, were forced to fall back exposing Riedesel's center. With a perfect view of Fraser's position, Morgan and Dearborn were able to surprise Fraser's forces from the forest on the British right. The British line under Fraser was forced back under the unexpected attack.

As the 24th fell back, some retreated to the Balcarres Redoubt. Riedesel had to deal with the attack by Learned from the center without support on the right or the left. As Learned's men began to advance, the British drums sounded as Riedesel commanded, "Fire!" The Germans were in two perfectly formed lines. Muskets from the front line cracked and sent a hailstorm of lead flying at the Patriot line. Some bullets sped past their heads or landed in the dirt at their feet, but others met their mark. Some were knocked back. Some fell in their tracks both forward and backward. Spattered Blood and shredded clothing flew through the air. Cries of pain and anguish echoed above the sound of gunfire.

Volley firing from the British center made immediate headway against Learned's center but could not hold back soldiers on the flanks who emerged from the woods to fire and then temporarily retreated to the protection of the woods to reload. The Americans did not feel obligated to accept the British rules of military engagement. Victory was their goal. No rules applied. With musket balls and grapeshot showering upon them, the Rebels responded on Riedesel's center from the field as well as from the cover of the forest. Smoke and fire shot from the muzzles of their guns. A volley of bullets into the Redcoat line instantly cut down several men. As the sound of cannon fire and gunfire echoed throughout the ravine, smoke billowed into the air creating a screen, partially blocking the view of the combatants. Gagging on the thick odor of burnt powder and sulfur, the Patriots reloaded.

Men on both sides, loyal and faithful soldiers, were baptized by human blood and adorned the ground hallowed by their human sacrifice. Soldiers howled for help or screamed in pain as grapeshot raked them, and their cries echoed throughout the ravine. Sounds of artillery and musket fire were mixed with the cries of pain of dying men and the helpless whinnies and cries of wounded horses. Hooves thundered across the wheat fields. Drums beat out orders. Charges were made, driven back, then made again sometimes with greater commitment and success, but sometimes not.

"Fire!" commanded Learned. "Hold the line! Fire! Hold the line!"

The American forces responded with a fury, shouting, firing, and thrusting their bayonets, hitting their targets with success as they advanced! Several times during the ensuing battle, the British center line was broken, but rallied to punish the American forces, driving them back. Lines swayed backward and forward on both sides like waves in the ocean. As soon as one side appeared to have the advantage, the other side would regroup and surge forward. The British could gain no permanent advantage. Whenever they were driven back, the Americans regrouped and came at them, stronger each time it seemed.

The Germans fought heroically, but the odds were too great. As the Americans rallied, the Hession line fired one last volley before retreating to the protection of the Balcarres Redoubt. The artillery backup fired several wagon loads of ammunition before the cannons became too hot to load, but it was too late to influence the battle. Though fighting with order and gallantry, before the drum corps could beat out the order, the Germans were in retreat. The Germans joined the melee of their left and right in retreat and made their way back to the Great Redoubt.

With the retreat of the British center and left and many from the 24th, General Fraser was on his own. He was Burgoyne's last hope and only he could save the day. Backing up Fraser, Burgoyne was tall, visible, and very prominent with musket balls striking his hat, his waistcoat, and one of his horses. Fraser, astride his handsome grey mount, with his sword held high in the air, rode back and forth reassuring the men of the light infantry, the remainder of the 24th, and the men retaking the field from the redoubts. He was able to rally them into a second line, slowly but surely forcing the Rebels to retreat.

When the battle began, Benedict Arnold mounted his horse and paced back and forth in proximity of the American lines in an ever-increasing state of agitation. Observing that the renewed effort and success by General Simon Fraser's forces was all that stood in the way of an American victory, he could stand it no longer. He had been held back too long by Granny Gates to be cheated of victory. Without orders or announcement, he spurred his horse into action and galloped onto the battlefield waving his sword and shouting, "Victory or death!" Hearing that Arnold had galloped toward the field, Gates concluded that he must have been drunk. He sent Major Armstrong in pursuit to order Arnold back to camp. Gates' thinking was that, regardless of the newfound success of Fraser's troops, the advancing darkness would ensure no less than a stalemate, leaving the business at hand to be restarted the next day after giving him and his officer's time to regroup and plan their next move. Seeing the messenger charging to his rear, Arnold outran him. Armstrong remained at the rear of the troops, having no interest in further pursuing a man who behaved more like a madman than a cool and discreet officer. Arnold pulled up alongside of Morgan and shouted to him.

"That officer upon a grey is of himself a host and must be disposed of!" Morgan nodded in agreement.

As the horse moved erratically from side to side, backward, forward, and up and down on its hindquarters with gun smoke fully surrounding Fraser and his mount, the smell of sulfur permeated the air. General Fraser waved his sword high above his head urging his men to attack the collapsing Rebel line.

From his many previous encounters on the battlefield, Arnold knew that if Fraser was hit, there would be a sudden pause in the attack on the retreating Americans, and an inevitable loss of morale by the British troops, a pause that he was not about to let go to waste. Anticipating this pause and loss of morale, Benedict Arnold's heart began to pound. As Timothy Murphy climbed a tree and positioned himself, resting his double-barreled Kentucky long rifle against a branch of the tree to steady it, he took aim at the moving target partially obscured by gun smoke some 300 to 500 yards away. Arnold waited with bated breath. Murphy fired and the shot missed wildly. The second was a near miss, appearing to strike the crupper at the rear of the horse's saddle. With the third shot, the general slumped forward and slipped off his mount to the ground!

With the fall of their leader, as Arnold expected, the British troops began to falter. Several British soldiers in near proximity to the general laid down their weapons to tend to their fallen leader. Observing the British halt of the advance and the sudden silence of British muskets, Arnold's heart beat rapidly with excitement. This was the moment he was waiting for.

"It is late in the day but let me have men and we will have some fun with them before sunset!" he shouted. Then, withdrawing a flask of rum from his chest, he threw back his head drinking a generous portion of rum. He sent Morgan and Dearborn on a wide outflanking movement to the west of the redoubts. Arnold galloped to the center directly between the fire of both the British and American of lines, somehow escaping from being hit. With his eyes flashing, observing also that the Germans had lost their support and were in retreat, Arnold was successful in urging Learned's brigade to follow him without any intervention by Learned. With his sword raised high into the air, he picked up part of Poor's brigade as well and rallied the men of both brigades. He charged from unit to unit shouting and cursing like a madman to galvanize them into action, shouting, "Attack! Attack! Forward! Forward! Attack!" Charging between the lines, once again Arnold somehow was able to escape fire from both. When a Redcoat attempted to bayonet him, he hacked him to death with his sword and beat off several other British bayonets before continuing on his path to another part of the field, driving and slashing as he went.

Arnold's hastily formed unit sent Balcarres, now in command of Fraser's regiment, reeling and overran two stockaded cabins, taking out the loyalists and Canadians holding them, on the way between the Balcarres and Breymann redoubts. His track brought him to the rear of the Breymann Redoubt on rising ground a few hundred yards northwest of the Balcarres Redoubt. Breymann's men were already defending their position from the Morgan attack at the redoubt's front when unexpectedly attacked by Arnold from behind and were thus almost completely surrounded. This opened Burgoyne's position from the right and rear. Breymann was killed and Arnold was hit, piercing his thigh, snapping the femur, and shattering the bone. In the same round Arnold's horse was hit, killing it instantly. The thousand-pound animal collapsed onto Arnold's leg, further snapping the bone in several places. As nausea waved over him, on the verge of passing out, adrenalin enabled him to continue giving orders as he lay on the ground. With the battle already won, Arnold ordered the Hessian who fired the shot that struck him be spared saying, "Spare the soldier who did this. I hold no grudge. He was performing his duty." Just as the sun was setting Arnold was carried from the field.

When Fraser was hit, the heart went out of Burgoyne. Fraser was his friend and confidant and the type of leader whose troops would follow anywhere. As darkness fell over the landscape ending the day's fighting, the battle was over, and Burgoyne's army was saved from immediate disaster. Burgoyne knew he had to get what was left of the British forces back inside their lines. He sent word to Riedesel to cover the withdrawal of the British forces from the battlefield. There is no saying what may have happened had Arnold not been injured. General Benedict Arnold had many faults, but no one can deny that this battle was won because of his leadership, bravery, energy and, most of all, his keen insight into the reaction of the men of a fallen charismatic leader caused simply by the strike of a single gunshot at a critical time. That single gunshot was the catalyst that turned the tide in favor of the American patriots. Clearly General Benedict Arnold was the hero of the day!

<hr />

When Philip was within a few miles of his home, he could neither hear his wife's screaming nor his son's crying, but he could see smoke rising from where his little farmhouse stood. At first, he was befuddled. It could not be his house. This could not be happening again. Fraser said his house would be spared and his family protected. When his brain finally realized that the smoke was indeed rising above his little farm, a cold chill gripped him, and he became overcome, first with fear, and then with rage. He leaned suddenly forward in the saddle and urged the horse into a gallop.

Reaching the top of the knoll where the burning ruins of his home sat only twenty yards away, he leapt from the saddle and ran toward the smoking remains of his home, his eyes frantically searching for his wife and son. Lying directly in front of what once was the entrance to his house was the scalped body of his closest friend, confidant, and mentor, closer to him than any blood relative, staring into the sun. He knelt on one knee beside Drew's body, closed his eyes, and peeled back his shirt to cover his face. Then, suddenly, within several yards from where he knelt, he saw Renee's body lying face down, her skull covered in blood, deplete of her beautiful flowing jet-black locks. He rose to his feet and rushed to her side. Falling to his knees once again, he turned her body over. Her eyes were wide open as if staring into space. He closed her eyes, tore her apron from her waist, and covered her head.

And then this man who had never shed a tear in his adult life, still on his knees, buried his head in his hands as he lowered his head to the ground beside his beloved Renee and sobbed uncontrollably. After a few brief moments, as if controlled by some remote power, but actually controlled by something deep within his soul, he suddenly stopped his sobbing, lifted his head and arched his neck toward the sky and opened his eyes. His eyes were burning from the tears as he squinted in anguish through the sunlight and stared at the puffy cumulus clouds floating just beneath the blue sky.

"My son, my son!" he cried.

The words burnt into his mind, before he could even turn around to search for Robert, the gentle cries of a small child fell softly upon his ears. Not taking any time to wipe the tears from his face, he rose and followed the cries frantically searching for his son. Suddenly, looking down, there he was, nestled within the protective body and four legs of Soldat, both encircled by waist high weeds beneath a tree but ten yards from the burning ruins. Soldat had dragged the boy into the brush beneath the tree by grasping his clothing at the nape of his neck with his teeth. The dog whined, looking up at Philip as if fully aware of what had just occurred, but did not move. Philip lifted his son and held him with one arm while he hugged the dog around the neck with the other. Soldat whined and vigorously licked Philip's face. Philip rose and carried Robert to his horse. Cradling his son in his arms, he mounted his horse. The horse sauntered for a few yards, and then urged on by Philip, the horse broke into a gallop. Philip lowered his head, holding the reins with one hand and holding his son between his body and his arm with the other. Soldat followed behind. Philip raced up the river road as fast as possible toward the Pearsons.

Dismounting quickly but carefully cradling his son, he climbed the steps and banged on the door crying, "Martha, Martha, come quickly."

Martha appeared at the door almost immediately and was shocked to behold Philip's expression, showing something between fear and rage.

"Take him. I must go. It's Renee. They have killed her, and they have killed Drew. I must go," he muttered desperately thrusting the child into her arms.

Not waiting for a response, he leapt from the steps and onto the saddle in what appeared as an almost singular motion. He spurred the horse into a gallop as he sped down the river road toward the distant sounds of cannons in the distance. The sounds of battle intensified until it was apparent to Philip that it originated from directly west opposite the Freeman farm just below the Great Ravine. He dismounted and led the horse on foot about fifty feet, working his way through the trees where he ultimately tied the animal to a sapling. He made his way through the forest, musket in one hand, his pistol in the other with his tomahawk secured in his belt. When he reached a small clearing after about fifteen minutes, he climbed an Oak tree. Peering through the branches, Philip could see smoke about five hundred feet away in the heart of the Freeman's farm.

He climbed down from his perch and reached the edge of the open field working his way along the field's edge from tree to tree.

The sounds of battle grew louder and louder, and the smoke grew thicker and thicker. As he reached the battle site, he could see bodies of both the British troops and the colonial soldiers and militiamen strewn across the open field. Dropping to his stomach, he crawled on his knees and elbows to the body of the closest fallen British soldier. He rolled him over and removed his coat. Struggling to put it over his clothing while staying as close to the ground as possible, he managed to robe himself in the soldier's red coat and his tri-fold hat without being seen. He crawled back to the tree line and worked his way north until he was directly opposite, and between only 30 to 40 feet away from the British troops. As he watched the ebb and flow of the action, crouched behind a tree, he realized suddenly that he really had no plan of action. All he was aware of was that his head was spinning with thoughts of what had occurred back at his farm. His anger grew into rage as his heartbeat so hard that he felt it might burst from his chest. He became delirious as his heart pounded, pressing his rifle against his chest and his back against a tree.

Finally, Philip composed himself enough to continue observing the battle unfold before him. He observed General Fraser pulling back on the reins of his horse, raising the beast into the air on his hind legs as he implored his troops to advance. Fraser's horse raised into the air on its hind legs. As the horse moved erratically from side to side, backward and forward, and up and down on its hindquarters with smoke fully surrounding Fraser and his mount, the smell of sulfur permeated the air. Fraser waved his sword high above his head urging his men to attack the collapsing Rebel line. Philip leaning to left of his protective tree, observing the scene. His head cleared and he intuitively knew why he had come to this spot, perhaps only by fate. Dropping to one knee, raising his musket and leaning it against the tree to steady it, he aimed directly at the General's chest and fired within a fraction of a second of the discharge of the sharpshooter Timothy Morgan's weapon. Philip's shot struck General Fraser directly in the abdomen. As the general slumped forward and slipped off his mount to the ground fatally wounded, Benedict Arnold galloped to the center not realizing it was Philip's shot from ten yards that had struck the general, not Murphy's from over three hundred yards.

As he watched the demoralized British regiment retreat before his eyes, Philip felt a sense of calm. It was not as if he felt this act was retribution for Renee's death, but some reason, he felt he had just done the right thing. He had killed a second man in a period of only a few hours after the first, but this time he did not feel morally guilty of murder as he did after the first. He did not feel imprisoned by his conscience. Perhaps it was because of Locke's point, as Drew had reminded him, which not joining either side in a conflict always favored the side of the aggressor, or perhaps it was something else that he could not define. In any event, he felt free from any feeling of guilt or wrongdoing. Yes, he felt sure that he had done the right thing! As the battle moved away from his sight with the British in retreat, darkness began to fall. Appearing that the Rebels now had the upper hand, neither becoming further involved in the battle or following the retreat to watch its now obvious conclusion, Philip retraced his steps to Pearson's horse. He mounted the horse and proceeded at a steady pace toward the Pearson store, his mind struggling to determine what he would do now with a son with no mother and no home to which they could return.

He approached the store from the dock side since, with dusk approaching, Martha and young John would be in the living quarters entered from the door on the dock. As he came closer, he could see Martha's silhouette as she stood on the dock facing the sunset with John in her arms. As he drew closer, he subconsciously took note of her shapeliness and the beauty of her countenance. Of course, she was the beloved friend of both he and Renee, but he had always seen her as the little sister he protected to and from school. Now, suddenly he was seeing her for the first time as a woman. He climbed the steps to the dock, and also for the first time since helping Martha on the back of his horse on the way to and from school, Philip placed his arm around her waist. She smiled at him as she always did, and Philip bent to kiss his son.

He described what had occurred at his house, what he did at the battle, and how Soldat saved Robert. Then he dropped his eyes toward the ground for several seconds before raising them to face Martha.

"What am I to do now, Martha?" He asked sullenly.

"Why you shall stay here as you did before," she replied as if the answer was obvious. "Then, in your own time, you will rebuild your house. Robert will be fine with me. You know I will treat him as my own."

"I know that," Philip replied as he lowered his head and remained silent for several moments.

Although his heart was heavy with the loss of the wife he loved and cherished so much, he realized what he had to do. He raised his head, looking deeply into Martha's eyes.

"Martha, of the four people in my life who meant more to me than life itself, I have lost two within forty-eight hours. I cannot bear to lose the remaining two. God's house has many rooms, and Jesus has prepared a place for your father's, Renee's, and Drew's souls, but I must now care for their remains honorably and respectfully."

Martha knew that she and Robert were the remaining two people of whom Philip spoke. Philip stayed with Martha for the next several days. On the very first morning of his stay, Philip took the tools that he needed from the Pearson's and headed to his farm. There he cleared a small area in the woods behind the barn and dug two graves. He arranged for a carpenter-farmer from the settlement to construct two caskets and two engraved wooden crosses. With his help, Philip lowered the bodies of Renee and Drew, the two people he loved most in this world, into the earth and covered them with soil. Then, with just he, Martha, Robert, and Pastor Framingham present, and Soldat as well of course, a very private service was held one early morning just as the sun was coming up. As Pastor Framingham was beginning his final prayer, the sun emerged from behind the clouds and ribbons of sunlight slipped through the trees striking both graves directly, isolating them from all that surrounded them as if Philip had arranged that also.

During his stay, he, Sam, Pearson's friend, Ebenezer, and Martha were able to make arrangements for a proper service and burial for her father and Will Stanton behind the church. On the morning following Sam Pearson's and Will's burial service, after breakfast, Philip arose from the table and looked down at Martha still seated, holding Robert.

"I must help finish this thing we Americans have started, this fight for independence and the freedom we so cherish."

He retrieved his musket and attached his pistol and tomahawk to his waist and headed for the door. Martha followed him out the door and down the steps Robert in her arms. Soldat tagged along. At the bottom of the steps, Philip turned to face Martha.

"Please care for my son. I shall return."

Her heart aching, Martha could find no words. Philip bent and kissed his son. As he turned to retrieve his horse, after taking but a single step, he stopped suddenly, turned back, grasped Martha's idle hand, and then kissed her for the very first time, on her cheek. With no further words spoken, as Martha watched, holding Robert in her arms, patting him on the back as he whimpered softly, Philip quietly continued on his way toward his horse.

As he turned to wave, he observed Soldat following him.

"Soldat, no... Robert!" Philip commanded as he pointed to Robert and Martha who was now sitting on the bottom step holding the child. Soldat looked back at Robert and then back again at Philip.

"Robert!" Philip repeated still pointing.

Soldat turned and slowly walked back to Martha and Robert. He turned to face Philip and sat alongside the couple.

As Philip replied, "Good Dog," reassuring the dog in a quiet approving tone, Soldat turned toward Robert, licked the child in Martha's arms on his face, and lay down beside them. Philip turned, walked quickly to his horse, raised himself into the saddle and rode away without turning around again.

The British had suffered nine hundred casualties out of their force of 7,000 at this point, whereas the Rebels' numbers had grown to over 12,000 and casualties numbered only about 150. The next day

Simon Fraser was buried in the Great Ravine as he had requested on his deathbed. Gates did not press the attack further.

Recognizing the direness of his situation, that night Burgoyne ordered his troops to retreat to Ticonderoga sixty miles to the north. The march was almost unbearable proceeding through rain and mud with artillery rolling along behind them. The bateau rowed alongside the army in the river to the right. The mud created by heavy rain reached high above the ankles, sucking men in up to the top of their boots and causing the wagons to become stuck. A substantial number of the bateau fell into the hands of the American patriots. Late on the night of the 9th, the exhausted army stumbled into the fortified camp on the Saratoga heights they had constructed a month earlier. Burgoyne spent the night in the Schuyler house and the next morning had his men set fire to the house, burning it to the ground.

Over the next three days Burgoyne and his officers discussed their options and believing the escape route to the north was still available, decided to continue the retreat leaving the baggage and artillery behind. The three-day delay proved to be the downfall for Burgoyne. It had allowed time for the American's General Stark and his New Hampshire militia to seal off their escape route. His men were in no shape to engage well rested Continental forces in their path, but he still wished to delay a surrender as long as possible holding on to the hope that Clinton would arrive from the south.

However, General Clinton had plans of his own and it did not include traveling to Saratoga to rescue General Burgoyne. Clearly, General Clinton was not about to risk exposing the islands of Manhattan, Long Island, and Staten Island to rebel attacks. Burgoyne had been assured that Clinton would be heading north in time to meet the rebel forces from the south when he simultaneously would strike from the north. Instead, Clinton, along with seventeen hundred newly arriving reinforcements from England, headed on October 3rd, not to Albany as originally planned, but for the Rebel forts in the highlands of Pennsylvania. The British invasion from the north designed to end the war before it started was over.

Finally, on October 14th, with no signs of Clinton and realizing that his hesitation could only cause the situation to get worse, he sent a message to Gates concluding that he would propose "a cessation of arms during the time necessary to communicate the preliminary terms by which in any extremity, he and his army mean to abide." Over the next two days, in an agonizing process, several revisions of the terms were sent back and forth between the camps. Burgoyne and Gates ultimately agreed that the British troops would march out of their camp with the Honors of War and ground their muskets along the banks of the Hudson River. The troops were not to be considered prisoners of war and would be allowed to return to England on British ships. They must however agree to no longer fight in the present war with the Americans. The troops were to be quartered and fed at American expense until the return to England could be arranged. The officers were to be allowed to keep their carriages and horses and the Canadians allowed to return to Canada. However, Burgoyne urged his Loyalist colonial troops to escape to Canada, fearing for their safety at the hands of their captors. In the end, both sides finally agreed to the terms of what Gates had been calling the Articles of Capitulation. Reluctantly, as a final concession, Gates agreed to call the document a Treaty of Convention, or as Burgoyne interpreted it, an agreement between equals.

When Burgoyne did not respond in what Gates considered a timely manner, Gates finally lost his patience. He was about to reopen hostilities when the document arrived in Gates headquarters dated "Camp at Saratoga, October 16, 1777."

One month later, on the 17th of November, Burgoyne, in his best uniform, but without a trace of the Gentleman Johnny swagger, surrendered his sword to Gates who immediately returned it to him. The British troops marched to the appointed place by the river as agreed, laid down their arms at the feet of the Rebel troops lined in two rows. The American soldiers showed complete respect for their British counterparts.

Philip, now an enlistee of the Continental Army and a participant in the surrender as part of one of the two American lines, looked down the line and spotted General Schuyler's slave, Caleb, and Peter Framingham.

After the ceremony, Philip, Peter, and Caleb, all having noticed each other, sought each other out. Once Philip introduced Caleb to Peter, he explained what had happened to his family. He told them that his son was with Martha and explained how he came to be a member of the Continental Army.

"Have you seen Michael?" queried Peter.

"Yes, briefly. He was serving with British General Fraser," Philip replied giving no further details. "Caleb, how did you come to being a member of the Continentals?" "General Schuyler told me he would give me and Anna our freedom if I would sign up."

"And what will you do once this is over?"

"Really don't know, Philip, sir. We black folks is used to picking one row at a time," Caleb replied with a smile.

As they walked away from the scene, Philip, in the center, put an arm around each of the men. After a short distance they stopped.

"Peter, I am sure your father is very proud of you," Philip commented.

"As yours would be, Philip. Where are you headed?"

"I am headed to Pennsylvania with General Learned. And you?"

"I am heading to Rhode Island with General Stark." They both turned and faced Caleb.

"How about you, Caleb. Where are you headed?" inquired Philip.

"Don't know, haven't seen no action yet. Believe that be up to General Schuyler."

The men shook hands, said their goodbyes, and separated heading in different directions, looking back and waving as they did so. After a few steps, Peter shouted to Philip as he turned and walked backwards,

"Philip, we must pray for Michael, wherever he is."

"Yes, Peter, we must pray for Michael."

"All for one, one for all."

"Yes, all for one, one for all," Philip responded as the men turned and continued on their separate ways.

After the surrender, the British marched to Boston and were placed on ships to return to England.

The Surrender of General Burgoyne

by John Trumbull

1822

POSTFACE

Approximately ten months before the British surrender at Saratoga, the Continental Congress had named Benjamin Franklin an agent of a diplomatic commission by the Congress with the goal of attaining a formal alliance in support of the American cause of self-rule and independence from England. In France, Franklin was extremely popular among the scientific and literary communities, and some say even more popular with the ladies. A fur hat fashioned after the one he had brought from Canada and wore quite often became quite popular. While his fur hat became popular, and his personal achievements had gained him great acceptance and praise, his diplomatic success was slow in coming. Although the royal court would be happy to see their conqueror in the French and Indian War destroyed, they felt they could not declare formal allegiance to the colonies until they felt assured that the Americans were capable of being victorious over the British. Washington's defeat at Brooklyn and subsequent three retreats cast serious doubt on such by the court of Louis XVI. Franklin continued to press for a formal alliance, but of course, the Americans needed to start winning.

When the American's victory at Saratoga on October 17, 1777 reached Paris, it was celebrated as if it were a French victory.

As any true diplomat, Franklin did his best to be coy about America's need for military assistance. In contrast, the French began to aggressively pursue the alliance for fear the British would seek peace with the American colonies and thus prevent France from regaining territory in North America. Early in January of 1778, Louis XVI ordered papers be drawn to formalize this new partnership between nations. The victory accomplished what the trips to Canada and France by Benjamin Franklin could not, but as a result of the victory at Saratoga, Benjamin Franklin was received by the French Royal Court. One month later, on February 6th, the fledgling United States of America and the powerful France signed the *Treaty of Amity and Commerce* and the *Treaty of Alliance* in Paris, France, making the powerful French nation America's first ally. Although the war lingered on for four more years with numerous battles encompassing successes and failures on both sides from north to south, indeed it was this alliance that brought the final victory to the Americans in the final battle of the war at Yorktown, Virginia.

British General Cornwallis brought 8,000 British troops to Yorktown, Virginia during the Battle of Yorktown in the fall of 1781. They also expected help from British ships to be sent from New York, but the British ships never arrived! That was lucky for General George Washington and the Continental army. The thirteen colonies found their opportunity to beat the world's largest empire.

Early in October the French navy kept British ships from entering through the York River or the Chesapeake Bay. French troops led by General JeanBaptiste Rochambeau joined General Washington. Rochambeau and Washington thus gathered a combined army of 17,000 soldiers with the goal of taking Yorktown back from the British. The siege cut the British off from their supplies. After a while, the British ran out of food and ammunition. They could not continue fighting. After well over two hundred battles from north to south and exactly four years plus four days from the final victory at Saratoga, the British Empire surrendered to its rebellious colonies on October 11, 1781.

During the official surrender ceremonies, the Continental Army Fife and Drum Corps played *Yankee Doodle Dandy*.

The sound echoed over the proceedings as an anthem in tribute to those gallant warriors that fought, both those that lived and those who died, in this war for independence. Ironically, in doing so, the Patriots were also mocking those who had mocked them with the very same tune for the six plus years of the American fight for independence.

Saratoga was indeed the turning point of the revolution. It had been over six years from the first shots heard around the world at Lexington and Concord before independence could ultimately be delivered. Arguably, it could indeed be said that it was the single shot from the musket of Philip Eames, in not a watershed moment, but in a watershed second, which turned the tide of the Battle of Saratoga convincing France to come to the aid of the Americans that gave birth to the American nation.

EPILOGUE

As mentioned in my acknowledgments at the front of this book, this work was inspired by Hugh T. Harrington, specifically by an article he wrote entitled, *The Man Who Shot Simon Fraser: The Legendary Tim Murphy, Marksman of Bemis Heights*.

When I visited the Saratoga battlefield, now a National Historical Site, I took the tour which raised more questions than it answered about the events that occurred at this place in the autumn of 1777. After returning home, a few days later I googled the Battle of Saratoga on my PC and coming across this article by Mr. Harrington I became quite intrigued by it.

In it, Mr. Harrington points out that much of the written material about the battle credits sharpshooter Timothy Murphy with the shooting of British General Fraser, which subsequently contributed to the turning of the tide of the battle at Saratoga in the colonist's favor. However, the author points out that none of the many recorded accounts of the period mention the name of Timothy Murphy. There were no recorded primary witnesses to this action which for years has been credited to Murphy. In fact, it was first claimed that it was indeed Mr. Murphy who shot and killed General Simon Fraser some sixty-five plus years after the event, in 1845, by Murphy's own son. Author Harrington points out that although the authenticity of the claim has been questioned or rebutted by several researchers and historians since then, Timothy Murphy has been credited with the feat simply by it being reported as fact repeatedly by historians for over 245 years.

Some historians have claimed that Murphy was not even among the marksmen at the battle. Others have reported that Murphy, himself claimed that by the time he climbed a tree to shoot Fraser, that Fraser was out of sight. Mr. Harrington raises the question that, if Murphy did indeed shoot and kill Fraser, why was he not credited with it in his lifetime?

Further, Mr. Harrington questions himself the existence in 1777 of such a weapon with the accuracy and precision required to hit such a target at the distance described in early accounts, leaving the answer to that question to the experts. Even if it did exist, would the accuracy of such a weapon be so perfect that it could possibly hit a fixed target at the distance estimated to be 300 to 500 yards, much less a target blanketed by smoke and moving erratically in many different directions?

Mr. Harrington cites in his work a November 10, 1835 an issue of the *Saratoga Sentinel,* which was reprinted in William L. Stone's 1877, "The Campaign of Lieut. Gen, John Burgoyne and the Expedition of Lieut. Barry St. Leger," an October 7, 1835 letter from Ebenezer Mattoon, a lieutenant in a colonial artillery company during the battle. In his letter Mattoon states that the shot that killed Fraser did not come from Murphy's weapon. Mattoon reported that as he was helping a wounded officer leave the field of battle when he confronted an elderly man whom he saw shoot and kill General Fraser from a distance of about 198 yards with a long hunting gun. The letter stated that the old man said, "I have killed that officer, let him be who he will." Mattoon said that he replied to the man, "You have, and it is a general officer, and by his dress believe it is Fraser." Author Harrington goes on to cite additional evidence and arguments on both sides. His article is easily found by searching the internet, and I encourage the reader to check it out. I found it fascinating!

Obviously, many have pointed out that the fatal shot could have come from any participant in the battle who simply missed his target. In my novel, I have offered you my assertion of who fired the shot that gave birth to a nation, with as much evidence as historians have given for the person to whom they credit for firing the fateful shot after all these years since then, which is none!

Thank you, Mr. Harrington for the inspiration.

REDEDICATION

To my wife,

Martha,

and my children,

Maureen (anagram: Merneau) Renee Petkiewicz,

Andrew (Drew) Gerard Nazzaro,

and

Philip Eames Nazzaro

SOURCES

Once I had completed my novel, a fictional piece of work, the question of whether a bibliography was required arose in my mind. The last time I had to know the answer to this question was when I was in high school and college, well back into the previous century, and the answer at that time was quite definitive. So, in this age of technology, I was sure the answer was on the internet. It should not have come as a surprise that the answer would not be definitive at all, but it did.

In the case of a novel, the answer seemed simple enough and agreed to by all, some saying that a novelist is judged by his or her storytelling ability, not by his or her historical facts. However, there was not complete agreement regarding a historical novel.

I learned that some felt it important to give credit for others' work, but others felt a bibliography was an attempt to give credit to oneself for doing the research which is expected of a historical novelist. Some suggested it protected a writer from accusations of plagiarism. Others said a novelist is supposed to steal from his sources. Some writers said that some publishers required it, while others preferred a bibliography not be included, and others didn't care. My conclusion in this regard was that I had to decide for myself.

Since a historical novel attempts to intertwine fiction with historical fact, I think this can be confusing to the reader, and the reader should be able to check on what fiction is and what fact on his own is if he or she so desires. What makes it even more confusing is that many historical fiction writers intentionally change history for their own purposes, taking creative license. Finally, I have also found that sometimes there are different versions of the same event, all reported by different historians as fact.

In my case, I tried to confirm the historical events in my novel. If it does not agree with the reader's recollection or understanding of history, then he or she is invited to check my sources regarding what occurred at this time and place as well as other sources if they so choose. Therefore, I felt that it was important to give credit to the researchers and authors of the works I used as my sources. To each of these authors and researchers, I would also like to say that if I got it wrong in your view, I may have used a different source. Also, any misstatement certainly was not intentional, but may have occurred through oversight or error.

In conclusion, I decided that a pure literary bibliography was not necessary for a historical novel, but that a section called Sources would suffice. My conclusion was reinforced by reading Bill O'Reilly's '*Killing England.*' This work truly had more responsibility for historical accuracy than my fictional effort, so I concluded, if it works for Bill O'Reilly, it works for me. To help the reader separate fact from fiction, if interested, let me advise that, obviously any conversation between my fictional characters and historical figures is purely my creation. In addition, in conversations between some historical figures which my research revealed was not recorded, but did occur, the words exchanged between them in my novel were also my creation. These include the conversations between Benjamin Franklin and other commissioners to Canada and with members of the Continental Congress, conversation between General Gates and Benedict Arnold in Saratoga, and conversations between General Burgoyne and his reporting officers in the Schuyler house in Saratoga.

Note, in addition, in the event I could not locate the historical information I needed for context in hard copy, my default sources were the websites, wikipedia.org or history.com. With that said, my sources follow:

Garland, David. *Saratoga: A Novel of the American Revolution*. St. Martin's Press. 2005.

Harrington, Hugh T. *The Man Who Shot Simon Fraser: The Legendary Tim Murphy, Marksman of Bemis Heights*. Early American Review, Summer /Fall 2003. https://www.varsitytutors.

com/earlyamerica/earlyamericareview/volume7/ themanwhoshotsimonfraser.

History.com Editors. *Declaration of Independence.* https//www. history.com/topics/American-revolution/declaration-of- independence.

Hurley. Dr. Lance. *Christianity in America Come Back to Me.* Self- published. 2019.

Kelly, Martin. *Major Events that Led to the American Revolution.* https/www.thoughtco.com/timelineeventsleading toamericanrevolution104296. 2020.

Ketchum, Richard M. *Saratoga: Turning Point of the American Revolutionary War.* Henry Holt and Company. 1997.

Lunt, James. *John Burgoyne Battles of Saratoga.* Harcourt Brace Jovanovich. 1975.

O'Reilly and Dugard, Martin. *Killing England: The Brutal Struggle for American Independence.* Henry Holt and Company. 2017.

Phifer, Mike. *WARFARE HISTORY: John Burgoyne: Campaign to Saratoga.* https/www.warfarehistorynetwork.com.

Procknow, Gene. *Journal of the American Revolution: Franklin's Failed Diplomatic Mission.* https://allthingsliberty.com/2015/01/ franklinsfailed diplomatic mission/.

Saratoga. Park visitor's guide/pamphlet. National Park Service. 2015.

Schuyler House-Saratoga National Historical Park. https://www.nps.gov/ sara/planyourvisit/schuyler-house.htm.

The Thomas Swords Family. Saratoganygenweb.com. Wikipedia Editors. *Battles of Lexington and Concord.* https://en.wikipedia.org/ wiki/Battles_of_Lexington_and_Concord.

Wikipedia Editors. *John Stark*. https://en.wikipedia.org/wiki/John_Stark. Wikipedia Editors. *List of American Revolutionary War battles.*

https://en.wikipedia.org/wiki.org/wiki/List-of-American-Revolutionary-War-battles.

www.ingramcontent.com/pod-product-compliance
Lightning Source LLC
Chambersburg PA
CBHW021628120626
46545CB00002B/448